BASIC

BASIC

An Introduction to Computer Programming Using the BASIC Language

Revised Edition

by

William F. Sharpe
Nancy L. Jacob

THE FREE PRESS
A Division of Macmillan Publishing Co., Inc.
NEW YORK
Collier Macmillan Publishers
LONDON

The Free Press
A Division of Macmillan Publishing Co., Inc.
866 Third Avenue, New York, New York 10022

Collier-Macmillan Canada Ltd.

Library of Congress Catalog Card Number: 70-143518
Printed in the United States of America

printing number

6 7 8 9 10

Contents

Preface

In the last few years the electronic digital computer has been transformed from a device understood only by members of a small cult of worshipers to an indispensable part of the life of every student, scientist, and businessman. Universities have taken account of its importance with courses on computers, systems analysis, computer programming and more esoteric aspects of the field now known as computer science.

The key to an understanding of computers, and an essential skill for using them, is the knowledge of at least one computer programming language. There are many candidates. Some were developed when computers were both far more expensive and far less sophisticated than they are now. Such languages reduce the effort expended by the computer, but they often require substantial expenditures of time and effort by the user. Other more recently developed languages take account of current technology and costs but were designed for limited classes of problems. Still others were designed for professional programmers willing and able to learn and memorize rather complex sets of rules and restrictions.

This book describes a language that combines a number of desirable features with relatively few undesirable ones. The language is BASIC, developed at Dartmouth College under the direction of Professor J. G. Kemeny. It was designed for use with one of the first computer systems that allowed a number of people concurrently to communicate directly with the machine, using typewriter-like consoles. Since then, such *time-shared* computers have become commonplace. Many are available commercially, with costs as low as a few dollars per hour of use. It is literally true that a computer of this type is as near as the nearest telephone, because communication by means of standard telephone lines is the normal procedure for most commercial systems and many time-shared computers used by universities and private firms.

BASIC is the *lingua franca* for time-shared computer systems. But it is also found in more conventional environments, with the user preparing his instructions and data on punched cards and submitting them for processing as part of a batch of such jobs at a central computer facility.

This book is designed to allow the user to think of a computer as if the latter "understands" the BASIC language. Thus no details of any of the supporting systems are included. This makes the book particularly suited for those unable to use a computer system, because it allows them to concentrate on the computational and logical properties of a high-level computer language with relatively little concern for clerical details.

Very little is said about computers *per se;* the interested student is referred to any of the almost countless introductory texts or manuals on the subject.

BASIC can be approached on two levels—first, as a simple, yet powerful language for standard numeric processing; then as a rich language for efficiently describing a wide range of advanced applications involving both the manipulation of numbers and the manipulation of textual material. This book is organized to reflect the dichotomy. Part I provides a full description of the essential features of the language. It should suffice for those persons who are interested in obtaining an appreciation of computers, the ability to use them in their academic work, and/or sufficient understanding to communicate with computer people in later life. Part II is designed for those persons with deeper interests and/or the need to use computers for more complex tasks. It introduces procedures particularly useful to the mathematician or scientist (for example, matrix commands) as well as those particularly useful to the business student or social scientist (for example, string manipulation).

The average college student should be able to learn the material in Part I with five to ten hours of classroom exposure and an equal investment in time spent preparing actual programs. In many instances it may be both feasible and desirable to forego some or all of the classroom time, relying instead on this book and the availability of helpful advice when the student encounters problems or questions. In the final analysis the computer itself may be the best teacher.

This book is based heavily on our experience teaching computer programming at the University of Washington. It is a joint venture. Chapters

1 through 7 were originally written by one of us, then revised by the other. The roles were reversed for Chapters 8 through 13.

We believe that BASIC represents an excellent first (or only) language for most people to learn. It includes most of the logical and conceptual components found in other programming languages, while requiring a minimum of attention to housekeeping details. Moreover, students who have learned BASIC have little difficulty with other languages. The marketplace provided ample evidence of the usefulness of BASIC. We know no better test.

William F. Sharpe
Stanford University

Nancy L. Jacob
University of Washington

BASIC

Part I
Essential BASIC

Chapter 1

Introduction

The Computer and You

Imagine that you have a diligent, hard-working, and accurate, but totally unimaginative, clerical assistant. Since she (he, it) is so unimaginative, it is necessary for you to provide very precise sets of instructions (what to do) as well as data (what to do it to). To avoid any problems you and the assistant have agreed upon a rather limited language—vocabulary and grammar—for stating your instructions. The language has the virtue that it admits no ambiguity. If you follow the rules when stating your desires, the assistant will do precisely what you have in mind. If any mistakes are made, they will necessarily be yours.

Now substitue *computer* for *clerical assistant.* Call the set of instructions a *program.* Call the language BASIC. Otherwise everything is the same.

The object of this book is to teach the grammar and vocabulary of BASIC. Although no computer actually "understands" BASIC directly, virtually all modern computers have been taught (preconditioned) to act as if they do. The manner in which this was done need not concern the reader; for all practical purposes one can assume that such computers understand BASIC.

Communication

To make a computer do your work, you must provide it with a *program* (indicating what to do), *data* (things to be processed), and certain information required to identify you, to tell the computer how important you are, where to send the bill, and so forth. All of this must be sent to the computer somehow, and the computer must return information as well. Most installations provide users with typewriter-like consoles that can communicate with the computer either directly or over standard telephone lines. Others require that information be input from punched cards; output is then returned later on printed sheets. Detailed information about such matters obviously must be obtained from those in charge of the installation to be utilized. This book deals with the more essential and more general aspects—the writing of programs and the arrangement of data.

A program consists of a series of statements (instructions or commands); each is written on a separate line. The lines are numbered from top to bottom, with smaller numbers preceding larger numbers. Systems that allow the user to enter lines from a typewriter-like console keep the lines in correct numeric sequence, even if they are not entered in order. When using punched-card input, the user must usually arrange the cards correctly himself, with lower-numbered cards preceding higher-numbered cards.

Data are prepared in a similar fashion. Each line containing data is numbered, and the set of lines is arranged in sequence, either automatically (for console entry systems) or by the user (for punched-card systems).

Nothing will be said here about operating teletypewriters, keypunch machines, and so on. Such information is easy to obtain; the best method is simply to spend five minutes at a machine with someone who knows how to operate it.

Diagnostic Messages

As we have suggested, you can assume that the computer recognizes instructions written in the BASIC language. But what if you present it with an illegal instruction (*i.e.*, one that violates the rules for grammar and vocabulary presented in this manual)? In most cases the computer will be aware that it does not understand the instruction and make a reasonably well informed guess about the source of its (more properly, your) confusion. And it will tell you about its difficulty and provide its diagnosis of the problem. Don't be embarrassed by such *diagnostic messages;* most programmers learn more from them than from manuals.

Unfortunately the computer can detect only errors arising from illegal vocabulary and/or grammar; it cannot read your mind. If your program is constructed according to the rules, the computer will happily do precisely what you tell it to do. It is up to you to make certain that what you tell it to do is what you want it to do.

Output

When you give a program and data to a computer, one or two operations take place. First, the computer looks over your program. If serious errors are found, it tells you about them (with alarming candor, on occasion), and then it refuses to have anything more to do with you until you correct the errors. On the other hand, if it finds your program acceptable, it meekly begins to follow your instructions, looking at your data when told to do so and providing answers in accordance with your instructions.

Chapter 2

Getting Started

Here is an extremely simple program:

```
 10    REMARK -- PAYROLL PROGRAM
 20    REMARK -- PROGRAMMER, ROBBIE S.
 30    READ P
 35    READ H
 45    LET G = P * H
 60    LET W = .14 * G
 70    LET N = G - W
 80    PRINT P
 90    PRINT H
100    PRINT G
110    PRINT W
120    PRINT N
140    GO TO 30
```

A set of data to go with it might look like this:

```
900    DATA  2.25
901    DATA 40
902    DATA  3.00
903    DATA 41
904    DATA  2.97
905    DATA 35
906    DATA  3.10
907    DATA 49
```

Format

To make a program easy to read we often insert spaces in statements or indent some statements. Neither has any effect on the program; write it any way you choose. You might as well get used to capital letters; there are no lower-case letters on most input devices. Blanks may be inserted as desired; with one exception (described in Chapters 4 and 9), blanks have no effect on the meaning of a statement.

Line Numbers

Notice that each statement in the program has a line number and that the numbers are arranged in order. Line numbers are required and must be between 1 and 99999 in most systems. Only integers—whole numbers —are allowed. It is a good idea to leave gaps when assigning numbers (*e.g.*, writing 10, 20, 30, and so on) in case you subsequently wish to insert additional statements.

Remarks

Every statement must begin with a legal command (after the line number). The first two commands in the program at the beginning of this chapter are remarks. A remark is used to provide information for you and/or anyone else reading your program; it provides no information to the computer. In fact, the computer ignores remarks (saying, in effect, "He is only talking to himself, not to me"). To indicate a remark, simply use the command REM; after that you may write anything you please.

Remark

Instruction Sequence

A program is nothing more than a set of instructions (although remarks are instructions only in a rather academic sense). The computer is expected to follow the instructions in a particular order. If you are entering your program from a teletype or other remote terminal, the computer will execute your instructions sequentially by line number unless told to do otherwise. In other words it will first execute the statement having the lowest line number, then the statement having the next higher line number, and so on, unless the statements themselves tell the computer to deviate from that order. (The instruction in line 140 of our sample program does just that, as you will see.) Only *one* statement can be executed at a time. All this means you must be careful to assign line numbers that accurately reflect the order in which you wish the statements in your program executed. And the order of execution is the main reason why it is important to obtain a listing of your program with the statements appearing in order by line number (as has been done with all the programs in this book). It makes the program much easier for humans to follow, since execution will proceed from the top of the page to the bottom.

Variables

The computer is provided with a number of "mailboxes," each of which can hold a number. Each mailbox has a name. There are twenty-six mailboxes with simple one-letter names: A, B, C, . . . , Z. Some other mailboxes have two character names—a letter followed by a digit: A0, A1, . . . , A9, B0, . . . , B9, C0, . . . , Z9.

For convenience we often use the name of a mailbox to indicate the number in it. And because the number in a mailbox may be taken out and a new one put in its place, we often refer to the number in a mailbox as a variable (because it may vary as the program is executed). Thus variable A means the number currently in mailbox A; variable B3 means the number currently in mailbox B3.

Reading Data

The data on which a program operates often consist of a set of numbers. It is useful to think of the numbers as if they were in a stack similar to that used for dishes in many restaurants. At any given time there is a number at the top of the stack; when it is used (read) the next one pops up to the top of the stack.

The DATA statements in a program may be thought of as providing the stack of numbers for the computer. In this case the number 2.25 is at the top, the number 40 is next, and so on. The order is, as before, determined by the line number of the DATA statement; the DATA statement with the lowest line number will be the first to be used.

We are now in a position to understand statement 30 in the program. It says, "Take the number from the top of the data stack and put it in mailbox P, throwing away any number that might be there already." Thus after statement 30 has been executed the first time, the number 2.25 will be in mailbox P. It will have been "removed" from the data stack, leaving the number 40 at the top.

What happens when the computer encounters statement 35? The number from the top of the stack (40) is placed in mailbox H, and 3.00 is now considered to be at the top of the stack.

We often describe this process in more elegant terms. For example, we might say that the *value* 2.25 has been *assigned to* variable P. Or, more explicitly, we might say that 2.25 has been *read into* P. In any event the process is clear enough.

It should come as no surprise that P is being used to represent the hourly pay rate of some employee and H the number of hours he worked during the week. The object of the program is to compute his gross pay (G), withholding (W), and net pay (N). The computations are performed as specified by instructions 45, 60, and 70.

Expressions

Look at statement 45. The portion to the right of the equal sign is an *expression*. It specifies that certain *computations* are to be performed and a *value* obtained. To be specific, P * H says, "Multiply the number currently in mailbox P by the number currently in mailbox H; the result is the *value of the expression*." Notice that the numbers in P and H are *not* altered when the expression is evaluated.

Expressions are formed according to the standard rules of arithmetic. Five basic operations are available:

+	Addition
−	Subtraction
*	Multiplication
/	Division
↑	Exponentiation

Certain problems present themselves, however. Since the entire expression must be written on one line, ambiguities may arise. To divide A by the sum of B and C, you might say:

A/B + C

But this might be interpreted by the computer as the sum of A/B and C. It is possible to find out the rules the computer uses when there is an ambiguity, but why bother? Instead, just use parentheses to avoid any problems:

A/(B + C)

Expressions may be very complicated:

$$(C \uparrow (A3/(B * X))) - Z5$$

or very simple:

$$X4$$

They may use variables and/or *constants*. A constant is simply a number —usually restricted to have nine digits or less—written in the program. The rules for writing numbers apply to both constants and numbers included as data:

1. A decimal point may or may not be included.
2. A minus number is indicated by preceding the number with a minus sign.
3. A positive number need not be preceded by a plus sign.
4. Commas may *not* be included.

Some legal numbers are:

```
   .01
   .3
256.4
 35
 -1.257639
```

To summarize, an expression may be:

1. A variable or
2. A constant or
3. Any combination of variables and/or constants connected by operators, with parentheses included when necessary to avoid ambiguity.

When an expression is evaluated, the current values of the variables (if any) are used, along with the constants (if any) to obtain a single value (number). The values of the variables are *not* altered when the expression is evaluated.

LET Commands

The form of a LET command is:

LET *variable* = *expression*

It says, simply:

1. Evaluate the expression on the right-hand side of the equal sign.
2. Then insert that value in the mailbox (variable) indicated on the left-hand side of the equal sign, throwing away any value currently in the mailbox.

When the program reaches statement 45 for the first time, the current value of P (2.25) will be multiplied by H (40). The result (50) will then be placed in box G. The values of P and H are, of course, unchanged. After statement 45 has been executed, G will contain the gross pay for the individual being processed.

Statement 60 uses the value of G for further computation. It instructs the computer to multiply the current value of G (50) by .14; the result is then placed in box W. This is obviously the amount to be withheld.

Statement 70 calculates the individual's net pay (G – W) and inserts it in box N. The calculations are now complete.

PRINT Commands

It does little good to perform calculations if the results are simply left in the computer where no one can see them. Thus we instruct the computer:

```
80   PRINT P
```

This means, simply, "Print the number in box P." Printing has no effect on the contents of the boxes; it merely allows the user to see what the contents are. The full set of instructions:

```
 80   PRINT P
 90   PRINT H
100   PRINT G
110   PRINT W
120   PRINT N
```

causes the following numbers to be printed:

```
 2.25
40
90
12.6
77.4
```

Needless to say, this is hardly very elegant output. We will learn to improve it later; for the present be content with the ability to get numbers out of the computer and onto the output sheet where you can see them.

GO TO Commands

Although it is comforting to know that the computer has accurately processed the payroll for the first employee (the one making $2.25 per hour), it would hardly be worthwhile to write a program to do so little work. Had we wanted no more from the computer, we could have said:

```
140   STOP
```

But there are other employees to be processed; we want to tell the computer to do to them what it did to the first employee. To do this we simply instruct it to alter the normal sequence in which it follows instructions:

```
140   GO TO 30
```

This says, simply, "Go back to statement 30, then proceed again in order until I tell you to do otherwise."

What happens? The computer encounters statement 30, which instructs it to read the number at the top of the data stack (3.00) into location (variable, or mailbox) P; the former value (2.25) is thrown away in the process. The next statement instructs the computer to read the next data number (41) into H, and its former value is thrown away in the process. Then the computations are performed using the *current* values of P and H. Obviously the resulting values of G, W, and N will be those applicable to the new employee. For example, when statement 45 is executed, P * H (3.00 * 41) will be placed in G and the former value thrown away. Thus G will equal 123—the second employee's gross pay for the week. W and N will be computed similarly. And the final results (including P and H, shown for the records) will be printed on the output sheet.

After the second employee's payroll has been printed, the computer will again reach statement 140 and will once again go back to statement 30. The third employee's pay will be processed, then the fourth, then the fifth, and so on. When will it all stop? When the computer runs out of numbers. Obviously no more can then be done for you, so the computer will turn to someone else's job.

Reprise

For all its simplicity, the program shown here could be used to compute gross pay, withholding, and net pay accurately and rapidly for a great many (thousands, if you wish) employees. Every week you could prepare a new set of data and get a completely different set of results using the same program. Needless to say, there is more to the BASIC language; you will soon be able to do many more things (and to do them more elegantly). But it is useful to learn to crawl before attempting to run. Try to answer the problems at the end of this chapter. If you can't, reread the material before looking at the answers provided. Then write some programs of your own using the portions of the language you now know. The computer can help you.

Problems

1. Find any errors in the following expressions:

(a) 3
(b) X
(c) A0 + B3
(d) AB/C
(e) A + (B/C) * D
(f) −3 + X
(g) (8 + Z2)/−6
(h) A35 + C
(i) 3X/D
(j) (Q + I)W9
(k) ((A + B)/(C − X) ↑ 8
(l) 3 * (A/+8)
(m) A ↑ .5

2. What output would be produced if the set of data given for the payroll program (at the beginning of this chapter) were submitted with the following program?

```
  5 READ X
 10 READ Y
 15 READ Z
 20 READ Z2
100 PRINT X
105 PRINT Y
110 LET Q3 = X * Y
115 PRINT Q3
120 LET Z3 = Z2 - Z
125 PRINT Z3
150 GO TO 5
```

3. The value of a dollar at the end of N years compounded annually at an interest rate of 10 per cent per year is:

$$\text{value} = 1.10 \uparrow N$$

Write a program to read a set of values of N, producing for each one the value of a dollar at the end of that many years. Be certain to print N each time.
4. In a single LET statement, assign the value of the following expression to variable X:

$$\frac{Y + W}{\dfrac{Z}{(W * Y)} - \dfrac{(Y + 3)^2}{27.3}}$$

Be sure to use parentheses.
5. Write a complete program to do some sort of calculation, and prepare at least a few lines of data to test the program. When preparing your program:
   (a) Follow the sample program in this chapter fairly closely.
   (b) Limit your computations to relatively simple combinations of basic operations, using parentheses whenever there might be any ambiguity concerning your intentions.
   (c) Be certain that your program will terminate, either by reaching a STOP statement or by running out of data.
   (d) Try not to be too ambitious the first time. You may want to build confidence by merely copying the sample program and adding one or two extra computations and outputs.
   (e) If your program will not run, read the diagnostic messages from the computer, make the necessary corrections, and try again.
   (f) If the program runs but produces incorrect answers, play computer: Follow your own instructions until you find the error in your logic. Then correct the program and try again.

Answers

1.
   (a) This is perfectly legal; a constant is a valid expression.
   (b) This is legal, too; a variable is a valid expression.
   (c) This is legal; A0 is a valid variable name, as is B3. The value of this expression will be the sum of the numbers currently in boxes A0 and B3.

(d) Illegal. A is a variable name, as is B. If the programmer had meant to multiply A times B, he should have said so:

(A * B)/C

If the programmer thought that AB was a valid variable name, he needs to reread the chapter.

(e) This is perfectly legal; however, it is ambiguous. If the programmer intended to multiply D by the sum of A and (B/C) then he should have added some more parentheses, *e.g.:*

(A + (B/C)) * D

If you want to know what the computer will in fact do when there is ambiguity, the rules in most systems are

(1) Expressions inside parentheses are evaluated first.

(2) Within a set of parentheses (or, if there are none, within the entire expression):

a) all exponentiation (↑) is performed first, from left to right.

b) multiplications (*) and divisions (/) are performed next, from left to right.

c) additions (+) and subtractions (−) are performed last, from left to right.

Follow this set of rules to see how the computer would have handled the expression in this case if the programmer had *not* added more parentheses.

(f) This is legal; −3 is treated as a constant.

(g) This may or may not be legal, depending on the system used. The constant −6 conforms to the rules; however, the fact that the division operator (/) is next to the minus sign may cause a diagnostic message, because a minus sign is also used to indicate subtraction. To avoid such a possibility it is a good idea to throw in extra parentheses:

(8 + Z2)/(−6)

The general rule is to avoid situations in which two operators are next to each other.

(h) This is illegal. A35 is not a valid variable name. The computer will probably think that you have put a variable (A3) next to a constant (5). Whatever the computer thinks it has found, it won't like it.

(i) This is illegal, too. If the programmer meant 3 times X, he should have said so:

(3 * X)/D

(j) Same problem. Multiplication must be indicated explicitly:

(Q + I) * W9

(k) The parentheses fail to pair up here. To avoid this kind of error it is useful to check complicated expressions, using the following scheme. Read the expression from left to right, keeping a cumulative count. Start the count at 0. Whenever you find a left parenthesis—(—add one to the count. Whenever you find a right parenthesis—)—subtract one. The count should never become negative and should be zero when you reach the end of the expression. If not, you have made a mistake. If you don't find it, the computer will.

(l) As in (g), this expression may or may not be legal, depending on the system used, because the computer may be confused by the two adjacent operators. To cure this drop the plus sign, because it is redundant:

3 * (A/8)

(m) Perfectly legal. The value of this expression will be the square root of A.

2.

```
  2.25
 40
 90
 38
  2.97
 35
103.95
 45.90
```

3. There are, of course, many ways to write a program designed to accomplish any given task. The important point is to write one that works (whether or not it is "efficient" is clearly a secondary matter). A program to compute the values specified for this problem follows:

```
10    READ N
20    PRINT N
30    LET V = 1.10↑N
40    PRINT V
50    GO TO 10
```

4. Don't be afraid to use parentheses liberally. One way to write the statement is:

   LET X = (Y + W)/((Z/(W * Y)) − ((Y + 3) ↑ 2)/27.3)

5. Good luck.

Chapter 3

Conditional Transfers

The program in Chapter 2 was fine for determining pay and withholding for each individual on the payroll. Reduced to its fundamentals, the program looked like that shown in Figure 3.1, page 20.

This is a classic example of a *loop*—the main reason that it pays people to write computer programs. In essence we told the computer what to do for the first man on the payroll and then instructed it to loop back, read new data, repeat the computation, print the results, loop back, and so forth. The computer gets out of this loop by following the sensible rule that whenever it runs out of data there is nothing to do but give up.

The IF-THEN Command

You may not want the machine merely to stop after reading all the payroll data. Perhaps you would like to have it finish with a summary of the number of persons paid, total amount paid, and total amount withheld. To do this you need a *conditional transfer*—a statement that tells the computer to go (transfer) somewhere if (but only if) a certain condition is met.

Remember the way in which we set up the payroll data—each man's hourly pay rate was followed by the number of hours he worked during the week. After processing each man, the computer returned to process the next one. Our problem is to find some way to tell it when all the people have been processed. One way to do this is simply to add an unusual man at the end—one with an hourly rate of, say, −1 per hour, who worked, say −40 hours. Knowing that such a man will be the last in the set of data,

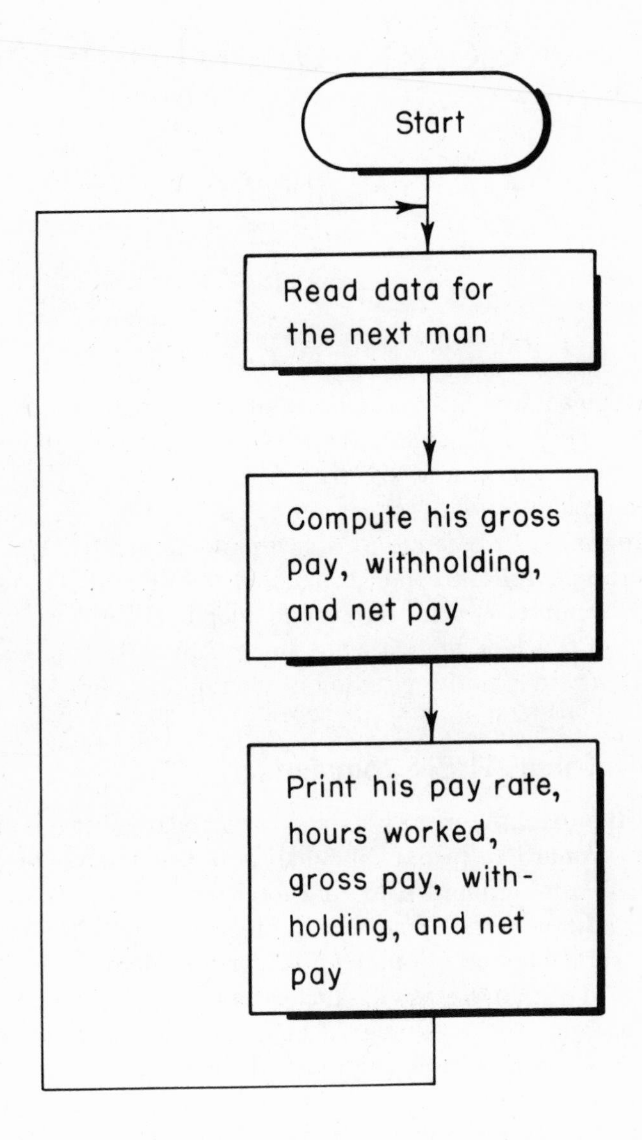
Start
Read data for the next man
Compute his gross pay, withholding, and net pay
Print his pay rate, hours worked, gross pay, withholding, and net pay

Figure 3.1

we can instruct the computer to watch out for him and to transfer to a set of instructions for preparing summary information when it encounters him.

The new arrangement is shown in Figure 3.2 on page 22.

After reading each pair of numbers, we tell the computer to look at the number it put in box P. If it is not negative, the numbers referred to a real man and are to be processed accordingly. But if the number read into box P was negative, the numbers did not refer to a real man; they were a signal to indicate that the last man had already been processed. When this condition takes place, we want the computer to transfer out of the loop and print the desired summary information.

The new program follows:

```
10    REMARK -- A MORE IMPRESSIVE PAYROLL PROGRAM
11    REMARK -- PROGRAMMER, DAVID MATTHEWS
12    REMARK
20    REMARK -- GET READY FOR PROCESSING
21      LET N1=0
22      LET T1=0
23      LET T2=0
25    REMARK
30    REMARK -- READ DATA FOR THE NEXT MAN
31      READ P
32      READ H
35    REMARK
40    REMARK -- TEST FOR COMPLETION
41      IF P < 0 THEN 100
45    REMARK
50    REMARK -- COMPUTE THIS MAN'S PAYROLL
51      LET G = P * H
52      LET W = .14 * G
53      LET N = G - W
55    REMARK
60    REMARK -- PRINT HIS PAYROLL
61      PRINT P
62      PRINT H
63      PRINT G
64      PRINT W
65      PRINT N
68    REMARK
70    REMARK -- ADD HIM, HIS PAY AND WITHHOLDING TO TOTALS
71      LET N1 = N1 + 1
72      LET T1 = T1 + N
73      LET T2 = T2 + W
75    REMARK
80    REMARK -- GO BACK TO READ MORE DATA
81      GO TO 30
90    REMARK
100   REMARK -- THIS POINT REACHED WHEN ALL MEN PROCESSED
101   REMARK
102     PRINT N1
103     PRINT T1
104     PRINT T2
105   REMARK
110     STOP
```

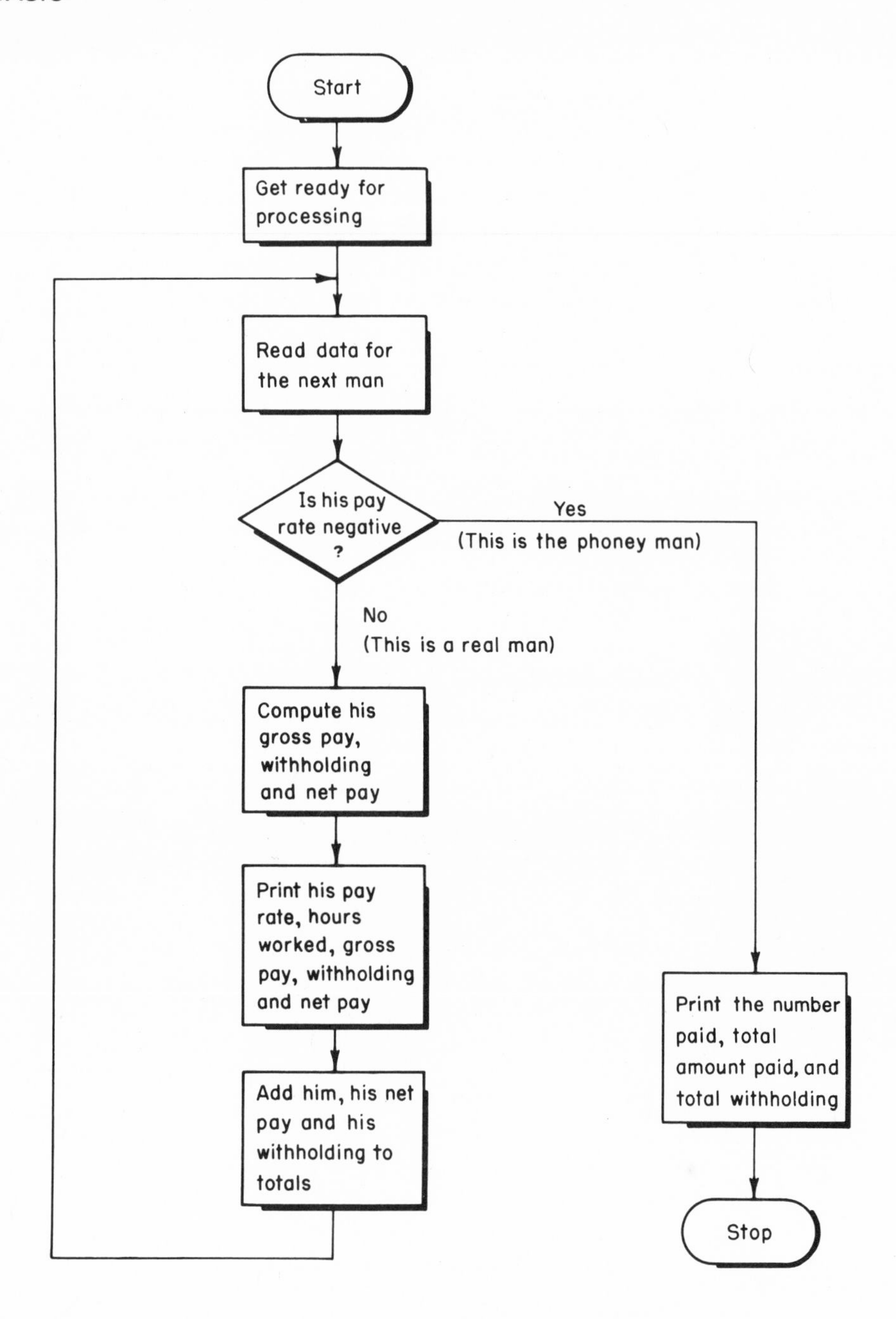
Start
Get ready for processing
Read data for the next man
Is his pay rate negative ?
Yes
(This is the phoney man)
No
(This is a real man)
Compute his gross pay, withholding and net pay
Print his pay rate, hours worked, gross pay, withholding and net pay
Add him, his net pay and his withholding to totals
Print the number paid, total amount paid, and total withholding
Stop

Figure 3.2

The conditional transfer in the program is:

```
41  IF P < 0 THEN 100
```

Its meaning is:

> If the current value of (the number in the box named) P is less than (<) zero, then go to line number 100. If it is not, proceed to the line that follows this statement (*i.e.*, number 45).

In general, a condition compares the values of two expressions. Of course, either expression may be simply a variable or a constant. Six types of comparison are possible:

Comparison	*Read as*
>	"is greater than"
<	"is less than"
=	"is equal to"
> =	"is greater than or equal to"
< =	"is less than or equal to"
< >	"is less than or greater than" "is not equal to"

The following examples illustrate the way in which the conditional transfer is used:

Statement	*Meaning*
IF A = G THEN 193	If the current value of A is equal to the current value of G, go to line number 193. If not, proceed.
IF A < > G THEN 503	If the current value of A does not equal the current value of G, go to line number 503. If it does, proceed.
IF N > 100 THEN 324	If the current value of N is greater than 100, go to line number 324. If it is not (*i.e.*, it is less than or equal to 100), proceed.
IF N > = 100 THEN 433	If the current value of N is greater than or equal to 100, go to line number 433. If it is not (*i.e.*, it is less than 100), proceed.
IF W < 5 THEN 234	If the current value of W is less than 5, go to line number 234. If it is not (*i.e.*, it is greater than or equal to 5), proceed.
IF W < = 5 THEN 235	If the current value of W is less than or equal to 5, go to line number 235. If it is not (*i.e.*, it is greater than 5), proceed.

The quantities to be compared may be very complicated expressions. But (as always) be certain to use parentheses whenever there might be any ambiguity. For example:

```
IF A > (B - C) THEN 500
IF (8 - C) * B < 34 THEN 200
IF (3 * A) - (B ↑ 2) = Q ↑ 8 THEN 300
```

You should also be sure there really is another statement in your program with the line number referred to by an IF statement; the computer may have no choice but to quit if it is told to go to a nonexistent statement.

As you may have noticed, all the IF statements appearing so far in this chapter have conformed to the following general structure:

IF *expression comparison expression* THEN *line number*

This structure is legal in all systems; therefore, you can be certain that IF statements written in strict accordance with it will be accepted by the computer. Modifications allowed by some systems will be discussed in Chapter 13; for now it is best to avoid any IF statement not fitting the structure.

The New Program

Initialization

Before the first man's payroll is processed, the number of personnel paid (to be recorded in box N1), the total amount paid out (to be recorded in box T1), and the total amount withheld (to be recorded in box T2) should all be zero. Statements 21, 22, and 23 set these variables to their initial values (zero). Statement 21, for example, says "Put the number 0 in box N1." Most loops are preceded by one or more such initialization instructions. Whenever a statement in a program refers to the current value of a variable (*e.g.*, by using it in an expression), the variable should either have been previously initialized to some value by a LET statement or have been assigned a value from data by a READ statement. The computer may balk at trying to evaluate an expression when you have not told it what value to assign to one of the variables. In some systems the computer merely takes the value to be zero; in others, it will complain to you and then quit.

Reading the Data

The READ statements are similar to those in the earlier program. The first time through the loop, the first two numbers from the data stack are read. The second time through, the next two are read; and so on.

Conditional Transfer

This is our new statement. If the numbers just read included a negative pay rate, the computer is supposed to go to line number 100. If not, it proceeds (to line number 45).

Computing and Printing Pay and Withholding

If the computer has read real payroll data into P and H, it will not transfer to statement 100 when it looks at P. Instead, it will proceed to compute the man's pay and withholding and print the results. The required statements (50 through 53 and 60 through 65) are, of course, similar to those used in the first payroll program.

Adding to Totals

After computing the pay and withholding for a new man, we want to record the fact that we have paid one more person. To do this we write:

```
71 LET N1 = N1 + 1
```

In essence this says:

> Take the number currently in box N1, add one to it, then put the result in box N1 (throwing out the previous value).

Obviously N1 is serving as a *counter*—every time a new man's pay is processed, N1 is increased (or stepped up) by one. When the last pair of numbers is reached and the computer transfers to statement 100, N1 will equal the total number of people paid.

The other instructions keep the cumulative sums of pay and withholding. The statement,

```
72 LET T1 = T1 + N
```

says:

> Take the number currently in box T1, add to it this man's net pay (N) and put the results in box T1 (throwing out the previous value).

When the last pair of numbers is reached and the computer transfers to statement 100, T1 will equal the total amount paid out.

The third statement (73) takes care of withholding; when statement 100 is reached, T2 will equal the sum of the amounts withheld.

Printing Summary Information

The section of the program starting with statement 100 is reached only after a negative pay rate is read. The next three statements (102, 103, and 104) print the desired summary information. Since no more work remains to be done, we tell the computer to STOP.

Style

Some additional points are worth mentioning before leaving this example. First, notice the many remarks used to remind the reader of the programmer's intentions. If anything, there are too few remarks here. Good practice would dictate that the programmer identify the meaning attached to various key variables. For example:

```
15   REMARK--P = PAY RATE IN DOLLARS PER HOUR
```

Notice also the number of "empty" remarks used to space, or set off, different sections of the program. Finally, notice that some statements have been indented to help to show the relationships among groups of instructions. Because the computer generally ignores blanks, this does not affect the operation of the program, and it may help considerably when you (or someone else) try to reconstruct the logic.

These are good habits. They require relatively little time when you are writing a program, and they may save a great deal of time later on.

Multiple Conditions

We have seen that the conditional transfer can be used to branch to a desired point in the program if some condition is met. But you may want to branch if any one of *several* conditions is met. It is not possible in some systems to specify more than one condition per IF statement, so several IF statements may have to be used. Assume that a special procedure is required for employees with more than two dependents or with a gross pay exceeding $200 per week. If this special procedure begins at line number 300, the program could include the following statements:

```
100   IF D > 2 THEN 300
101   IF G > 200 THEN 300
```

Obviously a number of other conditions could be added. If any were met, the computer would transfer to line number 300. If none was met, it would proceed to the next statement (*i.e.*, the one following the last IF statement).

Take another case. Assume that a procedure is to be followed if (and only if) a number of conditions are all met. For example, the amount to be withheld might be zero if an employee had more than three dependents *and* earned *under* $100 per week. If both conditions are not met, some alternative procedure beginning with line number 250 is to be followed. This situation can be represented in a manner similar to that shown in the previous example:

```
201  IF D < = 3 THEN 250
202  IF G > = 100 THEN 250
203  LET W = 0
```

By carefully arranging conditional transfers, you can represent virtually any type of multiple condition. As always, it pays to check the logic by playing computer, following your instructions with test data to insure that they do what you want them to do.

Problems

1. What is wrong with this set of instructions?

```
100    IF G < 200 THEN 120
110    LET T = .14 * G
120    LET T = 0
130    LET N = G - T
```

2. The computer is in the midst of a program. At the moment, the current values of key variables are

A	3.5
B3	−5.6
Z	100.2
Q2	0
F	1
K	−4.2
T9	100.2

For each of the following statements, decide whether or not the computer will transfer to statement 500:

(a) IF A > F THEN 500
(b) IF A < F THEN 500

(c) IF B3 < K THEN 500
(d) IF Z < T9 THEN 500
(e) IF Z < = T9 THEN 500
(f) IF Q2 > B3 − K THEN 500

3. Under what conditions (*i.e.*, for what values of A and B) will the following program segment assign the value one to variable T?

```
 10    IF A <= 50 THEN 90
 15    IF A > 100 THEN 90
 20    IF B <= 50 THEN 90
 25    IF B > 100 THEN 90
 30    LET T = 1
 35    GO TO 100
 90    LET T = 0
100    PRINT T
```

4. The rules actually followed when computing the amount to be withheld for federal income tax are rather involved. The amount to be withheld depends on: (a) whether the taxpayer is single or married; (b) the number of exemptions he has claimed; and (c) the amount he earns. Assume that the data to be processed include the following information for each employee (in the order specified): (a) his hourly pay rate; (b) the number of hours worked during the last *two* weeks; (c) the digit 0 (if he is single) or the digit 1 (if he is married); and (d) the number of exemptions he has claimed. The following tables indicate the rules that might be used by a typical firm.

Single Persons—Including Heads of Household

If the amount of wages during a two-week period (after allowing $29.20 for each claimed exemption) is		The amount of income tax to be withheld shall be	
Not over $8		0	
Over	*But not over*		*of excess over*
$8	$29	14%	$8
$29	$50	$2.94, plus 15%	$29
$50	$183	$6.09, plus 17%	$50
$183	$367	$28.70, plus 20%	$183
$367	$458	$65.50, plus 25%	$367
$458		$88.25, plus 30%	$458

Married Persons

If the amount of wages during a two-week period (after allowing $29.20 for each claimed exemption) is		The amount of income tax to be withheld shall be	
Not over $8		0	
Over	*But not over*		of excess over
$8	$50	14%	$8
$50	$183	$5.88, plus 15%	$50
$183	$367	$25.83, plus 17%	$183
$367	$738	$57.11, plus 20%	$367
$738	$917	$131.31, plus 25%	$738
$917		$176.06, plus 30%	$917

Write a program to read the information on each employee and compute the amount to be withheld from his income for the two-week period.

5. Make up some data to go with the program you wrote when answering problem 4. Be sure to include at least one person falling in each of the categories indicated in the rules for withholding. Then run your program and check its results with hand computations. This will prove to be time-consuming, but it constitutes an acid test of your program. It will also give you a real appreciation for the power of the computer (and the advantages derived from being able to program it).
6. Now program something that interests you. Be certain that your program will terminate either by reaching a STOP statement or by running out of data. Run the program with real or test data. And keep at it until the program really works.

Answers

1. Presumably the programmer wants to let T equal 0 if G is less than 200, and to let T equal .14 * G otherwise. The first goal is clearly met, but the second is not. To see why, assume that G is greater than 200. The condition in statement 100 is not met, so the computer proceeds to statement 110, which sets T equal to .14 * G. So far so good. But then the computer goes on to statement 120 which tosses out the current (desired) value of T and puts zero in instead. Obviously the computer should be told to skip statement 120 in this case. A solution to the problem follows:

```
100    IF G < 200 THEN 120
110    LET T = .14 * G
115    GO TO 130
120    LET T = 0
130    LET N = G - T
```

2.
   (a) 3.5 is greater than 1; the computer will transfer to statement 500.
   (b) 3.5 is not less than 1; the computer will not transfer to statement 500.
   (c) −5.6 is less than −4.2; the computer will transfer to statement 500. Think of numbers as lying along a scale:

   −5.6 −4.2 0 +5

   If one number lies to the right of another, we say it is greater; if it lies to the left, we say it is smaller.
   (d) 100.2 is not less than 100.2; thus the computer will not transfer to statement 500.
   (e) 100.2 is not less than 100.2, but it is equal to it; as long as either is true, the computer will transfer to statement 500.
   (f) Zero is greater than $-5.6 - (-4.2) = -1.4$; the computer will transfer to statement 500.
3. The conditions are that both A and B must be greater than 50 but less than or equal to 100. The program establishes that these conditions are met by a process of elimination; if either A or B has a value outside the acceptable range there is no further checking.
4. There are many possible ways to program this. The version shown below is just one of them. After data for an employee are read (statements 10 through 13), his gross pay (G) and taxable income (T) are computed. These computations are required for all employees and are thus performed first. Next the employee's taxable income is checked to see if it exceeds $8.00 (statement 26). If not, his withholding is set to zero, and the computer is instructed to go directly to the section for final processing (beginning with statement 200). If taxable income does exceed $8.00, the computer is told to see if the employee is married or not (statement 31). If the employee is married, processing begins with statement 100; if not, processing begins with statement 40. In either case the income bracket is found by *successively checking to see if T is less than increasingly larger* amounts. To see why this works, consider a single employee with a gross income of $100. The

computer will not transfer to statement 50 when it follows the instruction at statement 41. The mere fact that statement 42 is reached thus guarantees that his income exceeds $29. But if his income is not less than or equal to $50, the computer will proceed to statement 43. The fact that statement 43 is reached indicates that the employee is single and has an income greater than $50. If his income is also less than $183 (as we assume it is in this case), the computer will transfer to statement 70, which indicates the relevant amount to be withheld. Then the computer is told to transfer to the final portion of the program (located at statement 200).

The general procedure for finding the appropriate amount to be withheld is to pass through a number of IF statements involving less and less stringent requirements. When the appropriate bracket is found, the condition will be met and the computer will transfer to the relevant instruction. If none of the tests is met (*e.g.*, if the employee is single and earns over $458), the statement following the last IF statement will be reached.

The final section of this program simply computes the employee's net pay, prints the results, and then transfers back to process a new employee. These operations are the same for all employees and are thus written only once.

```
 1   REMARK -- WITHHOLDING PROGRAM
 2   REM
 5   REMARK -- READ DATA
10     READ P
11     READ H
12     READ M
13     READ E
15   REM
20   REMARK -- COMPUTE GROSS PAY AND TAXABLE INCOME
21     LET G = P * H
22     LET T = G - (29.20 * E )
23   REM
25   REMARK -- SEE WHETHER TAXABLE INCOME EXCEEDS 8 DOL
26   IF T > 8 THEN 30
27     REMARK -- NO WITHHOLDING REQUIRED
28     LET W = 0
29     GO TO 200
30   REMARK -- WITHHOLDING REQUIRED, SEE IF MARRIED
31   IF M = 1 THEN 100
35   REM
40   REMARK -- EMPLOYEE IS SINGLE, FIND BRACKET
41   IF T <= 29 THEN 50
42   IF T <= 50 THEN 60
43   IF T <= 183 THEN 70
44   IF T <= 367 THEN 80
45   IF T <= 458 THEN 90
46   LET W = 88.25 + ( .30 * (T-458) )
47   GO TO 200
50   LET W = .14 * (T-8)
```

```
51   GO TO 200
60   LET W = 2.94 + ( .15 * (T-29) )
61   GO TO 200
70   LET W = 6.09 + ( .17 * (T-50) )
71   GO TO 200
80   LET W = 28.70 + ( .20 * (T-183) )
81   GO TO 200
90   LET W = 65.50 + ( .25 * (T-367) )
91   GO TO 200
95   REM
100   REMARK -- EMPLOYEE IS MARRIED, CHECK BRACKET
101   IF T <= 50 THEN 110
102   IF T <= 183 THEN 120
103   IF T <= 367 THEN 130
104   IF T <= 738 THEN 140
105   IF T <= 917 THEN 150
106   LET W = 176.06 + ( .30 * (T-917) )
107   GO TO 200
110   LET W = .14 * (T-8)
111   GO TO 200
120   LET W = 5.88 + ( .15 * (T-50) )
121   GO TO 200
130   LET W = 25.83 + ( .17 * (T-183) )
131   GO TO 200
140   LET W = 57.11 + ( .20 * (T-367) )
141   GO TO 200
150   LET W = 131.31 + ( .25 * (T-738) )
155   REM
200   REMARK -- COMPUTE NET PAY AND PRINT RESULTS
201   LET N = G - W
202   PRINT P
203   PRINT H
204   PRINT G
205   PRINT W
206   PRINT N
210   REM
211   REMARK -- RETURN TO PROCESS NEXT MAN
220   GO TO 5
```

Chapter 4

Reading and Printing

By now you should be able to do rather esoteric types of computations; but the way you get data into the computer and, more importantly, the form in which you get answers from the computer are still likely to cause you some embarrassment. This chapter will expand your ability to control such operations. Although you will not be able to do things as elegantly as a professional might, you will be able to use convenient forms of input and to produce readable output.

Data

As we have seen, you can think of data numbers as if they were in a stack similar to that used for dishes—when the top one is removed (by a READ statement), the next one pops up to the top. To make this arrangement as vivid as possible we have included just one number in each DATA statement. But this is not necessary at all. You may include as many numbers as you wish; just separate them with commas. The numbers will be "stacked," or ordered, by reading the first DATA statement (the one with the lowest line number) from left to right, then the second, then the third, and so forth.

For example:

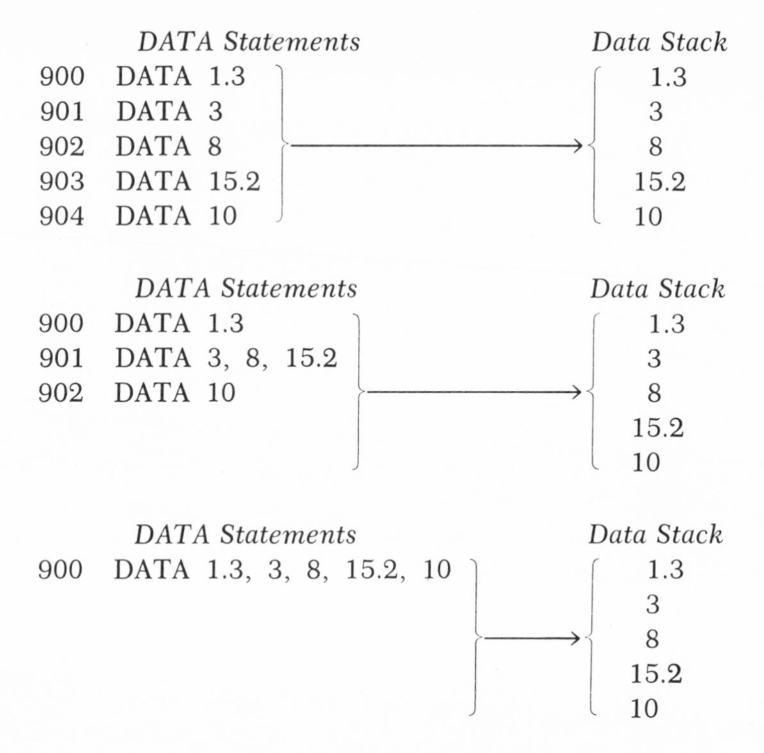

Obviously the way in which the user writes any given set of numbers is primarily a matter of convenience. However they are written, the numbers will be stacked in the order of their appearance (reading each DATA statement from left to right and all statements in order). Of course, only the ordering of numbers is relevant when the program goes to work.

DATA statements may be interspersed with program statements. However, to avoid confusion it is best to write them as a group after the last statement in the program.

READ Commands

Recall the way we have been writing READ commands:

READ P

This means "Take the number from the top of the data stack and put it in box P." To read two numbers in sequence we have said:

READ P
READ H

This is clearly a bother. The same thing can be accomplished by merely saying:

```
READ P, H
```

Would you like to read three values? Simply say:

```
READ X1, Y, Z9
```

This is precisely equivalent to:

```
READ X1
READ Y
READ Z9
```

You need only separate the names of the relevant variables with commas (so the computer will not get confused). Numbers from the data stack will be put in the boxes indicated (from left to right).

Often it is useful to coordinate READ statements and DATA statements. You might choose to put each employee's data in a single DATA statement,

```
DATA 2.10, 41, 1, 2
```

and read it with the statement:

```
READ P, H, M, E
```

But remember that the correspondence is strictly for your benefit. Any equivalent arrangement of READ statements and/or DATA statements would give the same results.

Strings

A string is a sequence of characters enclosed in quotation marks. The characters may appear in any order and may be letters, digits, and/or any of the special symbols available in your system. Some examples of legal strings are:

```
"HELLO"
"1600 PENNSYLVANIA AVENUE"
"MAY 31, 1970"
"* (A) + -$"
```

A string may contain blanks anywhere. The only character a string may *not* contain is a quotation mark; the computer requires that you use quotations only to indicate where a string begins and ends.

Strings may be used to print a message as part of the output of a program. For example:

PRINT "PAYROLL FOR JUNE, 1970"

The string will be printed exactly as you have written it, except that the quotation marks will not appear. This means that blanks *do* count in strings. In fact, blanks are relevant in a BASIC program *only* when they are inside strings.

There are other uses for strings in many BASIC systems. These will be discussed in Chapter 9. For now, the real advantage of strings is that they allow us to label our numeric output so that the meaning of the numbers printed will be clear to anyone.

Skipping Lines

Output produced with BASIC is single-spaced. If you wish, however, you may tell the computer to skip a line. To do this, simply tell it to print nothing:

PRINT

Printing the Values of Expressions

Thus far we have asked the computer to print only the values of variables. For example:

PRINT P

But you may ask for the value of any legal expression:

```
PRINT P
PRINT 3.5
PRINT A + 8
PRINT (X * 3) ↑ 8
```

The expression will be evaluated; then the value (number) will be printed. The computer will decide the best way to print it. Generally the number will be rounded to six significant digits (*i.e.*, the leftmost digit that is not zero and the five digits to its right), and then printed in a reasonably attractive manner. If the number is extremely large or extremely small, the computer may be forced to print it as a decimal fraction followed by E and an appropriate power of ten. Of course, none of this affects the values of numbers in the computer (*i.e.*, in the locations)—they remain in their original state.

Major Print Zones

Until now, we have printed only one number or string per line. You may wish, however, to condense your output by printing several items on each line. No problem. The output sheet is divided into print zones for just that purpose. You need only specify the zones in which you want your output to appear (*i.e.*, how you want the items spaced).

The output sheet is divided into five *major* print zones, each one fifteen columns wide. The computer always starts a new line in the leftmost zone and works its way right. How are print zones used? Suppose you want to print four numbers on a line. You could tell the computer to:

PRINT P, H, M, E

This says:

> Print the value of P (in the first major zone), then space and print the value of H (in the second major zone), then space and print the value of M (in the third major zone), and finally, space and print the value of E (in the fourth major zone).

Notice that the commas can be regarded as instructions to "space over to the next (major) zone of fifteen columns."

What if the computer runs out of zones, as in:

PRINT P, H, M, E, X1, X2

The answer is obvious: X2 will be printed in the first zone on the next line.

Remember that you can ask the computer to print the value of any expression. For example, an entire payroll program might be written as follows:

```
10   READ P, H
20   PRINT P, H, P*H, .14*(P*H), .86*(P*H)
30   GO TO 10
```

You may also include strings. They are printed starting at the beginning of the next available zone. If a string is longer than fifteen characters it will, of course, occupy more than one zone.

The output of the payroll program shown above could be improved by using strings:

```
 6   PRINT "PAY RATE","HOURS","GROSS","WITHHLDG","NET"
 7   PRINT
10   READ P, H
20   PRINT P, H, P*H, .14*(P*H), .86*(P*H)
30   GO TO 10
```

Here is how it will look (for the data values used in Chapter 2):

```
PAY RATE       HOURS          GROSS          WITHHLDG       NET

 2.25           40             90             12.6           77.4
 3              41             123            17.22          105.78
 2.97           35             103.95         14.553         89.397
 3.1            49             151.9          21.266         130.634
```

You can, of course, print both strings and numeric values on the same line. For example:

PRINT "PAY RATE = ", P

would produce this sort of output:

PAY RATE =   2.97

Notice that the comma itself is never printed. It serves only to tell the computer how to *space* the output. If you really want to print a comma for some reason, you'll simply have to print a string with one in it.

Minor Print Zones

The comma in a PRINT command allows you to print up to five items per line. But you may want to print more than five items on a line. Or you may want several items more closely spaced than one per major zone. What can you do? Use semicolons.

Each major zone is subdivided into five *minor* zones, each three columns wide. But the semicolon doesn't work on minor zones in exactly the same way as the comma works on major zones. Almost, but not exactly. To illustrate, let's look at the command:

PRINT A; B; X; Y8; W; Z3; V

This causes the values of all seven variables to be printed on the same line. Because a minor zone is only three columns wide, the computer cannot print the numbers from left to right in adjacent *minor* zones. You wouldn't be able to read the output. Many numbers are longer than three digits; and even if they were not, the output would be confusing without spaces between the numbers. Therefore, when *numeric values* are printed, the semicolon is really an instruction to "space to the first minor zone (to the right of the present location) that allows at least three spaces between the values." In other words when you use a semicolon, there will always be at least one full minor zone between the last digit of a number and the first digit of the following number.

Here's a sample program using semicolons:

```
10    PRINT 1;2;3;4;5;6;7;8;9;10;11;12;13;14;15
20    PRINT 16;17;18;19;20;21;22;23;24;25;26;27
30    PRINT 28;29;30
```

Its output looks like this:

```
1     2     3     4     5     6     7     8     9     10    11
12    13    14    15
16    17    18    19    20    21    22    23    24    25    26
27
28    29    30
```

As always, if you give the computer too many items in a single PRINT command, it will start printing at the left of a new line when it runs out of space. This is helpful, because it may be difficult to anticipate the exact number of items that can be printed on a line.

Strings may also be printed using a semicolon, but a semicolon after a string in a PRINT command is an instruction not to space *at all* after printing the string. This is handy. If you want to print two strings with no spaces between, you can. Or you can space them any way you want by adding blanks (inside the quotation marks, of course). Thus the command:

PRINT "THE PRESIDENT OF T";"HE UNITED STATES"

would result in the output:

THE PRESIDENT OF THE UNITED STATES

And the command:

```
PRINT "% ";"* ";"! ";"O ";"U ";"C ";"H "
```

would produce:

```
% * ! O U C H
```

In every other respect the semicolon acts like a comma. As before, you may print strings and expressions on the same line. And you may use both commas and semicolons in a single PRINT command. For example:

```
PRINT "PAY RATE=$"; P, " ", "HOURS WORKED="; H
```

would produce output like this: [1]

```
PAY RATE=$ 2.97              HOURS WORKED= 35
```

Notice that a "blank" string (*i.e.*, one with one or more blanks and nothing else) has been printed after the value of P. This is how "zone-skipping" is accomplished. You may skip minor zones this way, too.

The rules for spacing may seem confusing. But don't let them bother you. Just remember that the semicolon can give you closer spacing than the comma. For many applications the precise number of spaces between items is unimportant.

Dangling Commas and Semicolons

Normally the output generated by a PRINT command is begun at the leftmost margin of a new line. There is one exception, however. It arises if the previously-executed PRINT command ended with a comma or a semicolon. If it ended with a comma, the new output is started on the same line at the beginning of the next available major zone. If it ended with a semicolon, the new output is started at the beginning of the next minor zone that allows at least three spaces between numbers or, in the case of strings, at the very next column.

Confusing? It's really very simple. To illustrate, the commands:

```
PRINT A; B;
PRINT C
```

produce exactly the same output as the single command:

```
PRINT A; B; C
```

1. You may notice that in the output one blank space is left between "PAY RATE =$" and the value of P. Actually, this space is reserved for the sign (+ or −) of the number. Minus signs are always printed, but plus signs are not. Hence the blank.

As another example, the two programs below produce equivalent output.

Program A

```
10    READ P, H
20    LET G = P * H
30    LET W = .14 * G
40    LET N = G - W
50    PRINT P, H, G, W, N
60    GO TO 10
```

Program B

```
100    READ P, H
110    PRINT P, H,
120    LET G = P * H
130    PRINT G,
140    LET W = .14 * G
150    PRINT W,
160    LET N = G - W
170    PRINT N
180    GO TO 100
```

When might you want to use a dangling comma or semicolon? Perhaps you want to read in data items one at a time, but print them several to a line. For example:

```
10    READ A2
20    PRINT A2,
30    GO TO 10
```

The dangling comma tells the computer that the next print command *executed* should begin in the next major zone. This holds even when the next print command executed is the same one (being executed again during a subsequent pass through the program). Therefore, the output of this program will contain five numbers on all but possibly the last line (depending on the number of data items).

Problems

1. Find any errors in the following statements:
   (a) PRINT "NUMBER EARNING "BREAD" REGULARLY"

(b) PRINT A+B, C, "X =, X"
(c) PRINT 3; 5.8; 9
(d) READ A, B, C+D
(e) READ A, B,
(f) PRINT "ANNUAL PAY=$";25,300

2. Write a command that will print the word HELLO in the second major zone.
3. Write a statement to print the letter X in the center of the first major zone.
4. What output would be produced by the following program and data?

```
 10   READ X, Y, Z
 11   PRINT X, Y
 12   PRINT Z
 13   GO TO 10
900   REMARK--DATA FOLLOWS
901   DATA 3, 5.2, 8, 9
902   DATA 7, 10, 12
903   DATA 13, 15
```

5. What output would be produced by the following program?

```
50   LET I = 1
51   PRINT I,
52   IF I > 12 THEN 55
53   LET I = I + 1
54   GO TO 51
55   PRINT "     END"
56   STOP
```

6. What will the output of this program look like? (Don't bother to figure out the exact spacing between numbers.)

```
 10   LET T = 0
 15   READ A
 20   PRINT A;
 25   LET T = T + 1
 30   IF T < 7 THEN 15
 35   PRINT
 40   GO TO 10
100   DATA 25, 32.8, 9
101   DATA 12.5, 17
102   DATA 1.24, 35, 101, 13.259
103   DATA 12.3, 30, 2
104   DATA 51, 93, 86.5, 7
```

Answers

1. (a) Strings may not include quotation marks. The reason is obvious. The computer would regard this as two strings—"NUMBER EARNING" and "REGULARLY"—with the word BREAD trapped between them.

   (b) The statement is legal. The value of A + B will be printed in the first zone; the value of C will be printed in the second zone, and the string:

   X=, X

   will be printed in the third zone. Perhaps this is what the programmer intended. More likely he meant:

   PRINT A + B, C, "X=", X

   (c) This is perfectly legal because 3, 5.8, and 9 are all valid expressions (their values are, of course, 3, 5.8, and 9 respectively).

   (d) This is thoroughly illegal. You can read a number into box A and a second one into box B, but you cannot read a number into box C + D, because there is no such box. Numbers cannot be read into expressions; they can be read only into variables (boxes).

   (e) This is illegal. Commas are used to *separate* variable names in READ statements. The dangling comma is used *only* in PRINT statements.

   (f) This is legal, but the output may surprise the programmer. It will look like this:

   ANNUAL PAY=$ 25   300

   The reason is that the computer will interpret the comma as separating two numbers: 25 and 300. If the programmer intended to print a single number (25,300) with a comma in it, he should have said something like this:

   PRINT "ANNUAL PAY=$ 25,300"

   Commas may be embedded in a string, but *never* in a number.

2. This is an easy one. Just print a blank string in the first zone:

   PRINT " ", "HELLO"

3. Even easier. Just print seven blanks followed by X:

   PRINT "   X"

4.

3	5.2
8	
9	7
10	
12	13
15	

5.

1	2	3	4	5
6	7	8	9	10
11	12	13	END	

6. The first seven data values will be printed on line one; the second seven on line three. (The output is double-spaced owing to the PRINT command in line 35.) The remaining two numbers will appear on line five.

Chapter 5

Loops

One of the most useful techniques in programming involves the *loop*—the repeated execution of a series of statements with one or more changes made each time. Several loops have already been written; most programs contain so many that it is desirable to be able to write them succinctly. This chapter describes the FOR and NEXT commands. They allow you to replace several statements with two and, equally important, to make the structure of a loop much more obvious to anyone reading your program (including you).

FOR and NEXT

It is obviously senseless to repeat a series of statements unless something changes each time. Usually (but not always) the thing that changes is the value of some variable. In the typical case the variable is set at some *initial value,* and the relevant statements executed. Then the variable is changed (*stepped*) by some amount (up or down) and the statements executed again. Eventually the variable will pass some desired *terminal value;* at this point the computer is expected to proceed with the remainder of the program.

Assume that you want to compute and print the present value of a dollar at an interest rate of 5 per cent under various assumptions concerning the year in which the dollar becomes available. If it turns up in year N, the present value is

$$P = 1/(1.05 \uparrow N)$$

The following loop would compute and print the desired values for years 1 through 25:

```
10    LET N = 1
15    REM
20    LET P = 1 / (1.05↑N)
21    PRINT "   YEAR   "; N
22    PRINT "PRESENT VALUE ="; P
23    PRINT
25    REM
30    IF N >= 25 THEN 40
31    LET N = N + 1
32    GO TO 20
35    REM
40    STOP
```

In this case the variable that changes as the loop is executed over and over is N; its initial value is 1, its terminal value is 25, and the step is 1. Statements 10, 30, 31, and 32 take care of the housekeeping required to perform the operations in the desired manner. The loop itself consists of statements 20 through 25. When the looping is finished the computer is supposed to go to statement 40 (which is the end of the program in this case).

A simpler way to write the program is as follows:

```
10    FOR N = 1 TO 25 STEP 1
20      LET P = 1 / (1.05 ↑ N )
21      PRINT "   YEAR   "; N
22      PRINT "PRESENT VALUE ="; P
23      PRINT
30    NEXT N
35    REM
40    STOP
```

Not only are there fewer statements (two statements have replaced four), but the key information is contained in one statement (number 10), where it is more obvious to the reader (and to the programmer).

The statements comprising a loop written in this manner fall between the FOR statement and its associated NEXT statement. The variable to be altered when the loop is repeated is indicated in both statements, immediately after the command FOR and again after NEXT. The initial, terminal, and step values are indicated in that order in the FOR statement. The general form is this:

FOR *variable* = *initial value* TO *terminal value* STEP *step value*

Any or all of the three values may be indicated by expressions:

FOR X = A + B TO 3 * X STEP N

The STEP may be omitted; it will then be assumed to be one:

```
FOR Z = 1 TO 25
```

What does the computer do when it encounters a FOR statement? First, it sets the variable to the indicated initial value. Then it tests to see if it is already past the indicated terminal value; if so, it immediately transfers to the statement following the associated NEXT command. If not, the statements in the loop are executed. When the NEXT command is encountered, the computer adds (algebraically) the step value to the current value of the variable and tests again to see if it has passed the terminal value. If so, it goes on to the statements following the NEXT statement. If not, it goes back to the statement following the FOR statement. The process continues as long as necessary.

We have said (rather vaguely) that looping is terminated when the variable "passes" the specified terminal value. Just what does this mean? The answer is that it depends on the step being used. If the step size is positive, it means that the variable *exceeds* the terminal value (since the loop involves increasing values of the variable). If the step size is negative, it means that the variable is *smaller* (algebraically) than the terminal value (since the loop involves decreasing values of the variable). Needless to say, the step size should never be zero; this would imply that you wanted the computer to loop forever.

It is a good idea to avoid altering any variables mentioned in the FOR statement while you are in the loop. You may, if you wish, transfer out of a loop (with an IF or GO TO command). But you should avoid any subsequent transfer back into the middle of the loop unless no variables in the FOR statement have been changed in the meantime.

Loops may be nested inside each other. For example:

```
FOR I = 1 TO 10
    FOR J = 1 TO 10
        •
        •
        •
    NEXT J
NEXT I
```

They may *not* "cross" as in the following example:

```
FOR I = 1 TO 10
    FOR J = 1 TO 10
NEXT I
    NEXT J
```

All this may sound as if FOR-NEXT statements are more bother than they are worth. But in most cases you will find that they work quite nicely if you simply do what seems natural. The details indicated above to avoid possible problems are relevant only for cases in which a programmer attempts something exotic.

Examples

A few examples may be helpful. First, assume that you want to produce a table showing the present value of a dollar at 1, 2, 3, and 4 per cent when the dollar becomes available in years 1 through 25. One way of doing this is as follows:

```
10    REMARK -- HEAD TABLE
12    PRINT "         PRESENT VALUE OF A DOLLAR"
13    PRINT
14    PRINT "YEAR","1 PCNT","2 PCNT","3 PCNT","4 PCNT"
15    PRINT
17    REM
19    REMARK -- COMPUTE AND PRINT VALUES
20    FOR N = 1 TO 25
21      LET P1 = 1 / (1.01↑N)
22      LET P2 = 1 / (1.02↑N)
23      LET P3 = 1 / (1.03↑N)
24      LET P4 = 1 / (1.04↑N)
25      PRINT N, P1, P2, P3, P4
26      PRINT
27    NEXT N
28    REM
30    STOP
```

A slightly more compact way of writing it is the following:

```
10    REMARK -- HEAD TABLE
12    PRINT "         PRESENT VALUE OF A DOLLAR"
13    PRINT
14    PRINT "YEAR","1 PCNT","2 PCNT","3 PCNT","4 PCNT"
15    PRINT
18    REM
19    REMARK -- COMPUTE AND PRINT VALUES
20    FOR N = 1 TO 25
21      PRINT N,
22      FOR R = .01 TO .04 STEP .01
23        PRINT 1/((1+R)↑N) ,
24      NEXT R
25      PRINT
26    NEXT N
28    REM
30    STOP
```

In this simple approach, the inner loop spins R from .01 through .04 for each value of N from 1 to 25. Never again need you stand in awe of those massive tables of interest calculations found in so many reference books.

The next example illustrates the use of a loop to decrease the value of a variable. Assume that you want to read a number (call it N) and compute its factorial (F). The factorial of a number is found by multiplying it by itself less one, then by itself less two, and the like, until you get to one. In other words:

$$F = N * (N - 1) * (N - 2) * \ldots * 1$$

Now study the following program:

```
10    REMARK -- READ NUMBER, COMPUTE AND PRINT FACTORIAL
11    READ N
12    LET F = N
13    FOR M = N-1 TO 1 STEP -1
14      LET F = F * M
15    NEXT M
16    PRINT "FACTORIAL OF "; N; "= "; F
17    GO TO 11
```

See how it works? If not, play computer and follow the instructions with a number or two.

The final example is rather trivial. Assume that you want to skip five lines on the output sheet:

```
FOR K = 1 TO 5
  PRINT
NEXT K
```

Admittedly, the variable (K) is not used at all inside the loop. But who said that it had to be?

FOR-NEXT loops are extremely helpful when dealing with lists and tables. But that discussion must be deferred until the next chapter.

Problems

1. Find any logical errors in the following program segment (part of a program):

```
10    FOR Z = 1 TO 30
11      IF Z = 5 THEN 10
12      PRINT Z
13    NEXT Z
```

2. Find any logical errors in the following program segment:

```
10    FOR Z = 1 TO 25 STEP -1
11      PRINT Z
12    NEXT Z
```

3. Write a program to calculate and print the squares of the odd integers (whole numbers) from 1 to some number N. Arrange to have the value of N read in as data.
4. Write a program to compute the factorials of the numbers 1 through 10.
5. What output will be produced by the following program segment?

```
10    FOR N = 1 TO 5
15      FOR I = 1 TO N-1 STEP 1
20        PRINT " ",
25      NEXT I
30      FOR I = 1 TO 6-N STEP 1
35        PRINT I,
40      NEXT I
45    NEXT N
```

6. Write a program using the FOR and NEXT commands rather extensively. Keep at it until you are convinced that you understand how to use them.
7. Most computers do their calculations with binary numbers (*i.e.*, numbers to the base two, involving only zeros and ones). This can sometimes cause a problem when summing fractions. What kind of problem might arise, and how can it be solved?

Answers

1. The first time through the loop, Z will equal 1; the condition in statement 11 will not be met and Z will be printed. So far, so good. The second time through, Z will be 2. Again, no problem. The difficulty will arise during the fifth time through: Z will equal 5 and the condition in statement 11 *will* be met. The computer will then transfer back to the FOR statement and start all over again. This portion of the program will thus try to produce an infinite set of output consisting of the numbers 1, 2, 3, 4, 1, 2, 3, 4, 1, 2, ... Presumably the program-

mer meant to have the computer avoid printing Z when it is 5. If so, he should have told it go to the NEXT statement:

11 IF Z = 5 THEN 13

2. The step size here is negative. That means that the loop will be terminated as soon as the variable falls *below* 25. But its initial value (1) is already below 25. Thus the statement inside the loop (number 11) will never be executed.
3. Here is a possibility:

```
100    READ N
110    FOR I = 1 TO N STEP 2
120      PRINT "THE SQUARE OF "; I; " IS "; I↑2
130    NEXT I
135    REM
140    STOP
900    REMARK -- DATA
901    DATA 15
```

4. Simply modify the example shown earlier:

```
10    FOR N = 1 TO 10
12      LET F = N
13      FOR M = N-1 TO 1 STEP -1
14        LET F = F * M
15      NEXT M
16      PRINT "FACTORIAL OF "; N; "- "; F
17    NEXT N
20    STOP
```

Note that this program requires no data (no problem: just give it none).
5. This one requires some concentration. The output looks like this:

```
1    2    3    4    5
     1    2    3    4
          1    2    3
               1    2
                    1
```

If you didn't get this correct, play computer and go through the program again very carefully. Watch the FOR-NEXT loop in lines 15 to 25 particularly closely; when N equals 1 it doesn't get executed at all.

6. Never minimize the importance of writing actual programs and getting them to work correctly. It is the best way to learn programming.
7. Such complications rarely occur, but they can be irritating. The problem is the computer's inability to represent certain fractions with perfect accuracy as binary numbers (including some that can be easily represented as decimal fractions). Summing a number of such fractions may thus give a smaller total than expected. This should not be surprising, since it arises even with a desk calculator. For example:

$$\begin{aligned} &1/3 + 1/3 + 1/3 \\ &= .33333333 + .33333333 + .33333333 \\ &= .99999999 \end{aligned}$$

which is slightly less than one.

The solution is simply to anticipate the possibility. For example, instead of saying:

```
IF T = 1 THEN 100
```

say:

```
IF T > = .999999 THEN 100
```

Note, however, that this kind of problem can occur only with fractions (and only with certain fractions at that). By and large, you need not worry about it.

Chapter 6

Lists and Tables

By now you should realize that it is possible to store many different numbers simultaneously. You simply put them into different boxes (*i.e.*, give them different variable names). Numbers can be put into a box with a READ statement or a LET statement. And once a number is in a box it can be referenced in any expression (*e.g.*, in a LET, PRINT, or IF statement). But there is one problem that has undoubtedly plagued you already: If a group of numbers is to be stored concurrently, each must have a different name (*i.e.*, be in a different box). And the number of names is rather limited.

To overcome this difficulty and to allow more powerful techniques to be employed, programmers make extensive use of *lists* and *tables*. The general notion is simple. Imagine that you want to read and store the prices of eleven different products. You could say:

```
READ P1, P2, P3, P4, P5, P6, P7, P8, P9, R1, R2
```

But it would be much simpler if you could use a single letter to represent the type of information (*e.g.*, P for price) and then refer to the prices as P(1), P(2), ... Continuing with the analogy of mailboxes, you would refer to a box by its street (P) and the number on the street. Thus P(3) would refer to box 3 on P street, and P(11) to box 11 on P street. More relevant for our purposes, P(3) would refer to the third item in *list* P, P(11) to the eleventh item, and so forth. The use of such lists will greatly expand the range of problems that you can program easily. And the use of tables will expand it even further.

Lists

You may arbitrarily decide to use any letter for the name of a list. The particular item in the list is indicated within parentheses immediately following the name of the list. Thus:

A(3) is the third item in list A
Z(97) is the ninety-seventh item in list Z

Remember that a letter followed by a digit may *not* be used for the name of a list (or table, for that matter). Thus A9(3), for example, is quite illegal. Remember also to be consistent: Once you have appropriated a letter to serve as the name of a list or table you should not use it for anything else.

How many items may there be in each list? Unless you tell it otherwise, the computer will make provisions for a limited number (usually ten). How does it know that you have decided to use a particular letter for the name of a list? It looks over your program before going to work; if it sees a letter followed by parentheses it figures out what you are up to and acts accordingly.

You may refer to the number in a particular box in a list by giving the item number explicitly:

A(3)
A(65)

or implicitly, using any legal expression:

A(Z)
B(Q3)
C(A + (B * D))

When the item number is indicated implicitly, the computer:

1. Evaluates the expression inside the parentheses.
2. Rounds the result to the nearest integer (whole number).
3. Uses the appropriate item in the list.

It is imperative that you understand this procedure perfectly. For example, there is no such thing as A(I) or A(J); there is an item in box A(1), another in box A(2), and so on. Whenever the computer encounters A(I) during the execution of the program, it looks at the current value of I, substitutes it, and then finds the desired item in list A. To state it another way, when you refer to box A(I) in your program you are referring to an item in list A whose item number (position in the list) is stored in mailbox I. The following example illustrates the procedure.

Assume that at the moment:

$$I = 2$$
$$J = 4$$
$$K = 6$$

Then:

A(I) refers to A(2)— the second item in list A
A(J) refers to A(4)— the fourth item in list A
A(K) refers to A(6)— the sixth item in list A
A(I + J) refers to A(6)—the sixth item in list A

You may refer (explicitly or implicitly) to any item number in the list in question for which space has been reserved (of course you need not use all the reserved spaces). If you ever attempt to refer to an item for which space has not been reserved (*e.g.*, a negative item number or one exceeding the space reserved), the computer will complain.

The idea of a list is very similar to the notion of a subscripted variable used in mathematics. Thus the mathematician might write X_3 to indicate the value of the third of a series of variables named X. We would write this as X(3). For this reason we often call lists (and tables, too, for that matter) *subscripted variables*. Regular variables are thus *unsubscripted variables*, and they are quite different. Notice, for example, the difference between the unsubscripted variable P3 (the mailbox named P3) and the subscripted variable P(3)—the third item in list P.

One small point should be made here. In some systems the computer reserves a box for the zero-th item in a list; in others it doesn't. If you are in doubt, it is best to use only subscripts that are greater than zero.

Reading Data into a List

Assume that you want to read twenty-five numbers into a list named X. Now the FOR statement really comes into its own:

```
10   FOR I = 1 TO 25
11     READ X(I)
12   NEXT I
```

The first time through the loop, I equals 1. When statement 11 is executed, the computer reads a number from the data stack into box X(1)—the first box in list X. The second time through, I equals 2; the number is thus read into X(2)—the second box in the list. And so it goes, until all twenty-five numbers have been placed in their appropriate boxes.

Perhaps you want to read thirty pairs of numbers into lists X and Y; the first pair into X(1) and Y(1), the second pair into X(2) and Y(2), and so forth. This presents no problem:

```
10    FOR I = 1 TO 30
11       READ X(I), Y(I)
12    NEXT I
```

As a final example, assume that the first number in the data stack tells how many pairs are to be read. Then you simply write the following:

```
 9    READ N
10    FOR I = 1 TO N
11       READ X(I), Y(I)
12    NEXT I
```

Sorting Data

An important operation with lists involves sorting data into either increasing or decreasing order. There are many ways of doing this; we will use one of the least efficient (but most easily understood).

Assume there are thirty numbers in list X and you want to rearrange them so they will be in order, with the largest number first and the smallest last. The trick is to compare pairs of adjacent numbers. If the first one is larger than the second (or equal to it), the pair is acceptable. If not, the numbers should be switched. Obviously if all pairs are acceptable, the list is in the desired order. If not, it may or may not be. We thus want to pass through the list comparing all the adjacent pairs of numbers and recording the number of switches made. After completing a pass through the list, we check the number of switches. If none was made, the sorting is complete. If some pairs had to be switched, however, we pass through the list again to see if more switches are required. An example follows:

```
10    LET S = 0
11    FOR I = 1 TO 29
12       IF X(I) >= X(I+1) THEN 17
13       LET S = S + 1
14       LET Z = X(I)
15       LET X(I) = X(I+1)
16       LET X(I+1) = Z
17    NEXT I
18    IF S > 0 THEN 10
19    REMARK -- PROCEED
```

Note the way in which the switch is made. The number currently in box X(I) is stored temporarily in box Z. Then the number currently in box X(I + 1) is placed in box X(I). Finally, the number in box Z is placed in box X(I + 1). To see why all this is necessary, assume that:

$$I = 8$$
$$X(8) = 12$$
$$X(9) = 15$$

Now follow these instructions:

```
LET X(I) = X(I + 1)
LET X(I + 1) = X(I)
```

Obviously this would have disastrous results.

Note also that the FOR statement instructs the computer to let I = 1, 2, . . . 29. Why not let I equal 30? Because this would cause a comparison between X(30) and X(31); and we want to sort only the first 30 numbers in list X.

What would happen if the comparison had been written as:

```
12  IF X(I) > X(I + 1) THEN 17
```

Nothing, fortunately, if no two numbers were equal; but had there been at least one pair of numbers with the same value, the process could have continued indefinitely.

Finally, consider a problem in which you want to sort the values in increasing order. Just change the comparison to:

```
12  IF X(I) < = X(I + 1) THEN 17
```

Enough about sorting. It must be done with care, but it can be very useful.

Printing Numbers from a List

Assume that you would like to print the first N numbers from list X in a single column (*i.e.*, one number per line). Just write the following:

```
10    FOR I = 1 TO N
11       PRINT X(I)
12    NEXT I
```

If you would prefer to have the numbers printed in all five major zones (*i.e.*, from left to right on line 1, then on line 2, and so on), just add a comma:

```
10    FOR I = 1 TO N
11      PRINT X(I),
12    NEXT I
```

Recall that the dangling comma (or semicolon) tells the computer that the next print command executed should begin in the next available major (or minor) zone. Therefore, after the looping is completed it is a good idea to "clear" the system; otherwise the next print command (located somewhere else in the program) may begin its output in the middle of the page (*i.e.*, in the next available zone). The simplest way to accomplish this is to give the command PRINT after printing the numbers from the list:

```
10    FOR I = 1 TO N
11      PRINT X(I),
12    NEXT I
13    PRINT
```

Of course, there are many ways to print data contained in lists. Here is one last example:

```
10    PRINT "LIST P"
15    PRINT
20    FOR I = 1 TO M
25      PRINT "P(";I;") =";  P(I)
30    NEXT I
```

The output will look something like this:

```
LIST P

P( 1     ) = 37.4
P( 2     ) = 89.55
P( 3     ) =-12.2
```

Finding the Largest Number in a List

We can illustrate the points made thus far with a simple program designed to read a set of prices and to find the largest one. We assume that the first data number indicates the number of prices and that each price is followed by an identifying item number. The program is designed to find the largest price, then print it and the item numbers of all items with that price (there may be more than one).

The technique is relatively straightforward. Initially, the price of the first item is taken as the (temporary) maximum. Each price is then compared with the (current) maximum. If the new price is equal or smaller, no change is made; but if the new price is greater, it becomes the new (temporary) maximum. When all prices have been processed, the temporary maximum is clearly the real maximum. A second pass through the data is used to find the item numbers with that price. The program follows:

```
10    READ N
12    REMARK -- READ IN LISTS P AND I
20    FOR K = 1 TO N
21      READ P(K), I(K)
22    NEXT K
25    REMARK -- LOOK FOR MAXIMUM
30    LET M = P(1)
31    FOR K = 2 TO N
32      IF P(K) <= M THEN 34
33      LET M = P(K)
34    NEXT K
37    REMARK -- PRINT RESULTS
40    PRINT "MAXIMUM PRICE IS "; M
41    PRINT "ITEM NUMBERS FOLLOW "
50    FOR K=1 TO N
51      IF P(K) <> M THEN 53
52      PRINT I(K);
53    NEXT K
54    PRINT
60    STOP
```

Obviously the *smallest* price (and associated item numbers) could have been found if the comparison had been written as:

```
32  IF P(K) > = M THEN 34
```

Tables

Lists are very useful, but for some problems they are not enough. For example, you might be interested in ten cities. You could easily use lists to refer to the altitudes of the cities (*e.g.*, A(1), A(2), and the like) or to their populations (*e.g.*, P(1), P(2), and the like), but you might also want to refer to the distances between pairs of cities. For this you would need a *table*—one probably named D. The number in the third row and fifth column (showing the distance between city 3 and city 5) could be described most simply as:

D(3,5)

And that is exactly how it would be described. You may appropriate any (single) letter to represent the name of a table. The particular item in the table is indicated in parentheses, with the row number first and the column number second. The row and column numbers must be separated by a comma. Either or both may be indicated implicitly, using any legal expression:

```
D(3,5)
D(I,5)
D(I,J)
D(A+B,8)
D(3, X/Y)
D(A+B, X(I))
```

When an implicit row or column number is given, the computer evaluates the expression and then rounds the result to the nearest integer to determine the relevant row and/or column in the table. Both row and column number are checked to insure that space has been reserved for the item in question. If you do not explicitly reserve space, the computer will probably provide enough for you to use row numbers as great as 10 and column numbers as great as 10.

How does the computer know that you have decided to use a letter for a table? By looking over your program. If it finds a letter followed by a set of parentheses with a comma inside, it isn't very difficult to guess what you have in mind. But be consistent—if you decide to use a letter for a table name, do not use it for the name of a list (and vice versa).

Reading Data into a Table

To take a simple example first, let's suppose you want to set up a 3-row, 2-column table in your program, and you have prepared the entries for the table in DATA statements:

```
900  DATA 2.5, 33
901  DATA 19, 27
902  DATA 12.7, 5
```

The numbers are arranged so that each DATA statement represents one row in the table; statement 900 contains the entries for row 1, statement 901 contains the entries for row 2, and so on. The leftmost number in each statement goes in column 1 of the appropriate row; the rightmost number goes in column 2. How can we get all the numbers from the data stack into their respective places in the table?

It's easy. Let us first adopt some conventions. The name of the table will be R, and we will use the letters I and J to refer to a particular row and column, respectively, in the table. The following set of instructions reads in the first row of R:

```
10  LET I = 1
20  FOR J = 1 TO 2
30  READ R(I,J)
40  NEXT J
```

The first time through the loop, J equals 1, and the number 2.5 is read into R(1,1). The second time through, J equals 2, and the number 33 is read into R(1,2). But what about rows 2 and 3? We'd like to do the same thing over again with I reset to 2 and then, finally, with I reset to 3. By now, you have probably guessed what's coming next: another FOR loop, this one varying I from 1 to 3. The complete set of instructions to read in the table looks like this:

```
10  FOR I = 1 TO 3
20    FOR J = 1 TO 2
30      READ R(I,J)
40    NEXT J
50  NEXT I
```

And by modifying the terminal values in statements 10 and 20, you can read in any size table you want (provided sufficient space has been reserved).

One more example. Assume that you want to set up a table of distances for ten cities. Each set of three data numbers describes a direct route between two cities. For example:

```
900  DATA 3,5,275
```

indicates that there is a route connecting cities 3 and 5 and that the distance is 275 miles. In the table the number 275 should thus be entered in row 3, column 5 and also in row 5, column 3.

What about the distance from a city to itself? It is obviously zero. Thus D(1,1) should be set to zero, as should D(2,2), D(3,3), and so on. What about cities not connected directly? We want the table to show a very long distance (9999 miles, to be specific) for such cases.

The instructions required to set up the table are relatively simple. First all entries are set to 9999, except those along the diagonal (D(1,1), D(2,2), D(3,3), and so forth), which are set to zero. Then sets of data are read and the distances entered in the appropriate positions in the table (throwing out the previously entered values of 9999). The final set of data is assumed to consist of negative numbers, signaling the end of this phase of the problem.

The program segment follows:

```
10    REMARK -- SET UP 9999 VALUES AND ZEROES ON DIAGONAL
20    FOR I = 1 TO 10
30      FOR J = 1 TO 10
31        IF I = J THEN 35
32        REMARK -- THIS IS NOT ALONG THE DIAGONAL
33        LET D(I,J) = 9999
34        GO TO 37
35        REMARK -- THIS IS ALONG THE DIAGONAL
36        LET D(I,J) = 0
37      NEXT J
39    NEXT I
40    REMARK -- READ A SET OF DATA
41      READ C1, C2, M
42    REMARK -- TEST FOR A NEGATIVE NUMBER
43      IF C1 < 0 THEN 50
44    REMARK -- ENTER DISTANCE
45      LET D(C1,C2) = M
46      LET D(C2,C1) = M
47    REMARK -- GO BACK TO READ ANOTHER SET OF DATA
48      GO TO 40
50    REMARK -- PROCEED
```

If you find this difficult to understand, remember the advice given earlier: play computer. If a machine can understand these instructions, why not you?

Using Tables

The concept of a subscripted variable is actually quite simple. To understand it *perfectly* requires some diligence, but the effort is worth it. Once you have mastered subscripted variables, you will be able to write quite sophisticated programs using lists and tables. There are literally hundreds of applications. One is described below; you will, undoubtedly, think of others.

The example comes from security analysis. The data are the closing prices of shares of common stock on the last day of each of several months. Pick any ten stocks, then look up their prices for the last day of each of the past six months. You would then have sixty data values, one for each stock on the last day of a particular month. The values will be read into a table named S. The row in S of any item will be its stock number, and the column in S will be the month. Thus, S(4,6) refers to the price of stock 4 on the last day of month 6. Obviously, there will be ten rows and six columns in S.

We have selected common stocks and considered only sixty data values. But we could pick anything whose price or magnitude varies from time to time, use any time interval we wish, and have almost any number of values (within reason). The program should work just as well if we use the number of fish caught daily in each of five lakes during a one-week period. We would have to change only the number of rows and columns in S.

But back to stocks. Let's assume we're interested in knowing the following things about the data in S:

1. The average price (over the six monthly values) for each stock.
2. The standard deviation of the prices for each stock.[1]
3. The average price (over all stocks) for each month.

Here's the program:

```
10    REMARK -- SECURITY ANALYSIS PROGRAM
11    REMARK
12    REMARK -- SET UP NUMBER OF ROWS, COLUMNS IN S
15      LET N = 10
16      LET M = 6
17    REMARK
20    REMARK -- READ IN TABLE
21    FOR I = 1 TO N
22      FOR J = 1 TO M
23        READ S(I,J)
24      NEXT J
25    NEXT I
27    REMARK
30    REMARK -- PRINT HEADINGS
35    PRINT "SECURITY", "AVERAGE PRICE", "STD DEVIATION"
37    PRINT
38    REMARK
40    REMARK -- FIND AVERAGE PRICE, STD DEVIATION
42    REMARK -- FOR EACH STOCK
50    FOR I = 1 TO N
52      LET T1 = 0
55      FOR J = 1 TO M
57        LET T1 = T1 + S(I,J)
60      NEXT J
62      LET A = T1/M
63      LET T2 = 0
65      FOR J = 1 TO M
67        LET T2 = T2 + (S(I,J) - A)↑2
70      NEXT J
```

1. Standard deviation is the square root of the average squared deviations from the mean (*i.e.*, average) of a series of numbers. It will give an idea of the extent to which actual prices differed from the average price. If the standard deviation is very large, price varied quite a bit from month to month. If the standard deviation is close to zero, price remained fairly constant.

```
 72       LET D = (T2/M)↑.5
 74       PRINT I, A, D
 80     NEXT I
 82     PRINT
 84     PRINT
 86     REMARK
 90     REMARK -- PRINT HEADINGS
 92     PRINT "MONTH", "AVG--ALL STOCKS"
 95     REMARK
 97     PRINT
100     REMARK -- NOW FIND MONTHLY AVERAGES
105     FOR J = 1 TO M
107       LET T1 = 0
110       FOR I = 1 TO N
112         LET T1 = T1 + S(I,J)
115       NEXT I
118       PRINT J, T1/N
120     NEXT J
125     REMARK
130     STOP
```

Notice the way in which the loops are nested. In lines 50 through 80 the object is to compute the average price and standard deviation of price for each stock; thus the outside loop changes the value of I, which is used to indicate the row number. But in lines 105 through 120 the object is to compute the average price for each month; thus the outside loop changes the value of J, which is used to indicate the column number.

Reserving Space

In most systems, unless you explicitly reserve a specific amount of space, the computer will reserve enough for you to use subscripts as high as 10 for both lists and tables. Hence, references to P(10) and S(10,10) are perfectly legal even if you have not previously reserved space for list P and table S.

But you may want the computer to provide more or less space than this (more when you need more; less when you need less and the space is required for other lists and/or tables). To do this you indicate the desired dimensions explicitly in a DIM (for dimension) statement:

```
  10  DIM A(250)
 500  DIM B(3)
3150  DIM X(8,15)
```

The first statement reserves space for 250 items in list A. The second statement reserves space for three items in list B. The third statement reserves space for eight rows and fifteen columns in table X.[2] You may reserve space for more than one list and/or table with a single DIM statement; the entries are simply separated by commas:

```
5 DIM A(250), B(3), X(8,15)
```

DIM statements may appear anywhere in a program; the computer will find them before it goes to work. Remember, the space to be reserved must be indicated *explicitly*—no expressions allowed.

A Small Restriction

Generally you may use a subscripted variable (list or table reference) anywhere you are allowed to use a simple (unsubscripted) variable. There is one exception, however. The variable altered during execution of a FOR-NEXT loop should be an unsubscripted variable. This limitation refers only to the variable mentioned immediately after FOR in the FOR statement (and again after NEXT in the NEXT statement). The initial, terminal, and step values may involve any expression at all, including subscripted variables.

Problems

1. Table Z has ten rows and ten columns. Write a set of statements to set all the entries to zero.
2. What output will be produced by the following program?

```
10   FOR I = 1 TO 8
11      LET B(I) = 2 * I
12   NEXT I
20   FOR J = 1 TO 6
21      PRINT B(J),
22   NEXT J
30   STOP
```

3. What output will be produced by the following program?

2. Some systems also provide for 0 entries—A(0), B(0), and row 0 and column 0 for table X, in this example.

```
10    FOR K = 1 TO 4
11      LET Q(K,K) = 9
12    NEXT K
20    FOR K = 1 TO 4
21      FOR L = K+1 TO 4
22        LET Q(K,L) = 1
23      NEXT L
24    NEXT K
30    FOR K = 1 TO 4
31      FOR L = 1 TO K-1
32        LET Q(K,L) = 0
33      NEXT L
34    NEXT K
40    FOR K = 1 TO 4
41      FOR L = 1 TO 4
42        PRINT Q(K,L),
43      NEXT L
44      PRINT
45    NEXT K
50    STOP
```

4. Assume you have been given a program which reads in list X and sorts the numbers into ascending order. X has 50 items and has been previously dimensioned. Write a program segment (to add to the given program) which "moves" the items in X to another list Y, so that Y is sorted in *descending* order. When you are finished, you should still have list X in its original order. (Don't forget to dimension Y.)
5. Assume that you have been asked to expand the program given in this chapter for setting up the table of distances for direct routes between pairs of cities. Add the necessary instructions to find and print the shortest distance from city 1 to each of the other cities. Hints:
   (a) Let S(J) be the shortest distance from city 1 to City J.
   (b) To get started, let S(J) = D(1,J).
   (c) Now, assume that S(3) is the current shortest distance from city 1 to city 3, and that S(3) + D(3,5) is less than the current value of S(5); what would you do?
   (d) In general, assume that S(I) + D(I,J) is less than S(J); what would you do?

   Remark: This is a difficult problem. If you conquer it, you are well on your way to programming rather complicated procedures; however, even if you fail, the situation is far from hopeless.

Answers

1.

```
10    FOR I = 1 TO 10
11      FOR J = 1 TO 10
12        LET Z(I,J) = 0
13      NEXT J
14    NEXT I
```

It is good practice to "clear" lists and tables in this manner before starting processing. In some cases it is absolutely essential.

2.

```
 2     4     6     8     10
12
```

Remember that there is no B(I) or B(J); only B(1), B(2), and so on.

3.

```
9   1   1   1
0   9   1   1
0   0   9   1
0   0   0   9
```

If you didn't get this right, get out a piece of paper and play computer, doing exactly what the instructions tell you to do.

4. Would you believe?

```
1000    DIM Y(50)
1001    FOR I = 1 TO 50
1002      LET Y(51-I) = X(I)
1003    NEXT I
```

If you don't believe it, make up some phoney numbers, stick them in list X, and then see what the program does to them. This is, of course, just one of several ways (but a very efficient one, at that) to solve the problem.

5. The program statements through and including line 50 are the same as those shown in the earlier example. A possible set of additional statements to solve the problem follows:

```
51    REMARK -- SET UP INITIAL VALUES
52    FOR J = 2 TO 10
53      LET S(J) = D(1,J)
54    NEXT J
55    REMARK
60    REMARK -- CHECK EACH VALUE FOR POSSIBLE IMPROVEMENT
61    LET Z = 0
62    FOR J = 2 TO 10
63      FOR I = 2 TO 10
64        IF I = J THEN 69
65        IF (S(I) + D(I,J)) >= S(J) THEN 69
66        REMARK -- SHORTER ROUTE FOUND
67        LET Z = 1
68        LET S(J) = S(I) + D(I,J)
69      NEXT I
70    NEXT J
71    IF Z = 1 THEN 60
75    REMARK
80    REMARK -- PRINT RESULTS
82    FOR J = 2 TO 10
83      IF S(J) = 9999 THEN 86
84      PRINT "SHORTEST DISTANCE TO",J,"FROM 1 =";S(J)
85      GO TO 87
86      PRINT "CITY"; J; "CANNOT BE REACHED FROM CITY 1"
87    NEXT J
90    STOP
```

To see how the program works, use the following data:

```
901    DATA 1, 2, 10
902    DATA 1, 4, 50
903    DATA 2, 3, 90
904    DATA 2, 4, 30
905    DATA 3, 4, 40
906    DATA -1, -1, -1
```

Chapter 7

Functions and Subroutines

Functions

Periodically you may want to calculate some type of *function*. For example, you may want to find the logarithm of a number. Several of the more useful functions of this type can be obtained by simply asking for them. The function desired is usually indicated by a three-letter name. The value to be used is indicated explicitly or implicitly in parentheses following the function name. Thus LOG(8) refers to the natural logarithm of eight, and LOG(A + B) to the natural logarithm of the number found by adding A to B. The expression in the parentheses is called the *argument* of the function; it is evaluated and the resulting number used as indicated.

A function may be used in any expression. For example:

```
10  LET Z = A + LOG(3)
20  LET Q3 = A +(5 * LOG(3))
30  IF B + LOG(C) > 50 THEN 433
40  PRINT LOG(C)/LOG(B + 8)
```

When the computer encounters a function, it:

1. Evaluates the expression in the parentheses.
2. Applies the rules specified for the function in question (*e.g.*, takes the logarithm of the number).
3. Uses the resulting number as if it had appeared instead of the function name and its argument.

Ten of the functions available for the asking are described below. For convenience each is written here with an argument of X, but of course the argument may be any legal expression.

Function	*Gives*
LOG(X)	The natural logarithm of X
EXP(X)	The value obtained by raising e (= 2.71828. . .) to the X'th power
ABS(X)	The absolute value of X
SQR(X)	The square root of X
INT(X)	The integer part of X. For example: if X is 9.8, INT(X) = 9
SIN(X)	The sine of X; X must be expressed in radians
COS(X)	The cosine of X; X must be expressed in radians
TAN(X)	The tangent of X; X must be expressed in radians
ATN(X)	The arctangent of X; the arctangent is given in radians
SGN(X)	If X > 0, SGN(X) = 1 If X = 0, SGN(X) = 0 If X < 0, SGN(X) = −1

Random Numbers

A computer may be used to simulate events that happen in a somewhat random manner. One way to do this would involve reading in as data a list of random numbers. However, this is not necessary, for the computer acts as if it has its own list already (actually it computes numbers as required, but you need not concern yourself with such details). Each number in the list lies between zero and 1. If you were to produce a great many numbers, you would find that they fall rather uniformly over the range (in other words, they come from a uniformly distributed population of random numbers between zero and 1). You can get the next number from the list by simply asking for it in the following manner: [1]

RND(0)

This can appear in any expression; in form it is like the regular functions, although its value is obtained in a very different manner. When the computer encounters RND(0), it simply substitutes the next number from its list of random numbers and proceeds.

---

1. In most systems any argument may be given, because it is not used. A few systems produce different numbers, depending on the argument.

For example, the following program:

```
10    FOR I = 1 TO 5
11      LET Z = RND(0)
12      PRINT Z
13    NEXT I
14    STOP
```

might generate the following output:

.151432
.901628
.012963
.594318
.770312

To simulate the results obtained by flipping a coin five times, simply write the following:

```
20    FOR I = 1 TO 5
21      IF RND(0) <= .5 THEN 24
22      PRINT "HEADS"
23      GO TO 25
24      PRINT "TAILS"
25    NEXT I
26    STOP
```

Each time statement 21 is executed, a random number (the next one in the list) will be obtained; if it is greater than .5, the computer will print HEADS; if it is not, the computer will print TAILS.

Would you like a random number between 0 and 38? Simply write this:

```
10   LET R = 38 * RND(0)
```

Obviously 38 times a number falling between 0 and 1 must give a number between 0 and 38. If you would like R to be an integer between 1 and 38, simply write this: [2]

```
10   LET R = INT(1 + (38 * RND(0)))
```

2. In the unlikely event that the random number turns out to be exactly 1.0, this statement would set R to 39. To insure against this, you could follow line 10 with

```
11   IF R = 39 THEN 10
```

One problem may bother you. The first time RND(0) is encountered, the first number in the computer's random number list is substituted; the second time, the second number is substituted, and so forth. If you want to start at a different place in the list each time you run your program, merely tell the computer to look at some of the initial entries.[3] Then it will begin the real work with numbers lying farther down in the list. For example, preface the actual computations with:

```
10    READ N
11    FOR I = 1 TO N
12      LET X = RND(0)
13    NEXT I
```

and then put some arbitrary value for N in a data statement.

Subroutines

By now you have undoubtedly had the following experience: You have a procedure requiring several statements; moreover, the procedure needs to be followed in several places in your program. It is obviously a bother to rewrite all the statements repeatedly in every part of the program in which the procedure must be followed. You need some way to write the statements once and then refer to them as required. To do this you write the procedure as a subroutine. Whenever you want to execute it, you tell the computer to go to the beginning of the subroutine but to remember where it was before beginning the subroutine. When the statements have been executed, the computer is expected to return to the appropriate place in the program.

The two new statements required for subroutines are GOSUB and RETURN. GOSUB is similar to a GO TO: the difference is that when the computer is told to GO TO 200, it goes to line 200 and promptly forgets where it was when it transferred there. But when it is told to GOSUB 200, it transfers to line number 200 and remembers where it was prior to the transfer. Later, when the computer encounters a RETURN statement, it will automatically go to the statement following the GOSUB from which it transferred.

To illustrate the use of subroutines, assume that the following statements occur somewhere in a program:

---

3. Some systems make this unnecessary; a simple command (*e.g.*, RANDOMIZE) may be used instead.

```
200    LET F = N
201    FOR M = N-1 TO 1 STEP -1
202      LET F = F * M
203    NEXT M
204    RETURN
```

This is the routine to compute the factorial of a number. Now assume that you want the factorial of some number, for example, X3. You simply put its value in box N and call in the subroutine:

```
10    LET N = X3
11    GOSUB 200
12    PRINT F
```

When the computer reaches statement 11, it transfers to statement 200, making a note of the fact that it got there from statement 11. Statement 200 is then executed, and the factorial is computed by the statements following it. Eventually statement 204 is reached. The computer then returns to the statement following number 11—statement 12.

Perhaps you need to calculate the factoral of X8 at some later point in your program. Just say:

```
56    LET N = X8
57    GOSUB 200
58    PRINT F
```

This example illustrates another advantage of the subroutine. Once you have written a set of statements to compute a factorial and checked them out to insure that they work, you can regard them as a "little black box." Any time you need a factorial, just write GOSUB 200. This is extremely helpful when you are writing large programs. You simply break the program into modules that are logically distinct, programming each as a subroutine. In fact, it is not unusual to encounter programs that look like this:

```
10    REMARK -- READ DATA
11      GOSUB 100
12    REMARK -- PROCESS DATA
13      GOSUB 200
14    REMARK -- PRINT DATA
15      GOSUB 300
16    REMARK -- RETURN TO PROCESS ANOTHER SET OF DATA
17      GO TO 10
```

The statements required to perform the desired operations would then follow. Although the first statement in a subroutine can be of any type, it is good practice to let it be a remark indicating the purpose of the subroutine:

100 REMARK—SUBROUTINE TO READ DATA

There are many advantages to be gained if programs are written in this modular manner. It is even possible to have different people program different parts of a problem. Of course, there must be close coordination so that the same variable will not be used inadvertently for different purposes in different subroutines.

You may have GOSUB statements within subroutines. For example, consider the following (nonsense) program:

```
 10   READ N
 11   GOSUB 100
 12   PRINT Q, R, Z
 13   STOP
 20   REM
100   REMARK -- SUBROUTINE A
101   LET Q = 2 * N
102   GOSUB 200
103   LET R = Q / Z
104   RETURN
105   REM
200   REMARK -- SUBROUTINE B
201   LET Z = 8
202   FOR I = 1 TO N
203     LET Z = I * Z
204   NEXT I
205   RETURN
```

When statement 11 is reached, the computer transfers to statement 100. It soon reaches statement 102, which sends it to statement 200. Eventually a RETURN is encountered at statement 205, and the computer returns to the place from which it departed most recently (in this case, statement 103). Later, upon encountering another RETURN it goes to statement 12, as intended.

As with many other features in BASIC, there are some things to watch out for when using subroutines. Never allow the computer to "fall" into a subroutine without going there via a GOSUB, as in:

```
 10    REMARK -- MAIN PROGRAM
 20    READ P
 25    IF P > 0 THEN 40
 30    GOSUB 100
 40    PRINT P
 45    REM
100    REMARK -- SUBROUTINE
110    LET P = INT(ABS(P))
120    RETURN
```

Why not? Because when the computer comes to the RETURN, it won't know to which statement it should return. GOSUB is the only statement that provides it with a memory of where it has been.

Unless you know exactly what you are doing, never allow a subroutine to contain a GOSUB to itself. This is called *recursion*, and experienced programmers sometimes use it for special kinds of problems. But if "self-calling" subroutines are used inadvertently or without a thorough understanding of recursion, the computer may find itself in an "infinite loop" (*i.e.*, circling through your program forever).

Playing Roulette

Many of the points in this chapter are illustrated in the following program. We assume that a prospective gambler wishes to try certain strategies for playing roulette in a simulated casino. His betting strategy is called a *martingale*. He begins with a basic bet (B); whenever he wins, he returns to his basic bet. Whenever he loses, however, his next bet is double the previous (lost) amount—unless his money is insufficient, in which case he bets everything he has. The player continues until he either exhausts his capital or reaches some predetermined upper limit (U).

Our gambler is convinced that his martingale strategy is sound, but he is uncertain as to whether he ought to put his money on number 1 each time or on "red" (there are fifteen red numbers). If he chooses the former, he wins thirty-five times his bet if successful. If he chooses the latter, his successes will be more frequent, but he will win only an amount equal to his bet each time. The gambler wants to be able to indicate in his data which of the two playing strategies is to be simulated. He also wants to be able to indicate whether or not a complete record of results (spin by spin) should be printed.

The program is relatively straightforward. The roulette wheel is assumed to have thirty-eight numbers and to be fair. Notice the extensive use of subroutines. This makes it easy to make changes in the program; for example, to alter strategies, calculate the effects of unbalanced wheels and the like. Note also the use of P and S9 as "switches" to select the appropriate subroutines to be employed. Such techniques are essential for the professional programmer, and they can be valuable for you as well. The program follows:

```
 10    REMARK -- PROGRAM TO SIMULATE ROULETTE PLAY
 11    REMARK -- READ DATA
 12      GOSUB 100
 13    REMARK -- PERFORM INITIAL PROCESSING
 14      GOSUB 200
 15    REMARK -- SPIN WHEEL
 16      GOSUB 250
 17    REMARK -- FIND RESULTS (DEPENDING ON STRATEGY)
 18    IF S9 = 1 THEN 21
 19      GOSUB 300
 20        GO TO 22
 21      GOSUB 350
 22    REMARK -- PRINT RESULTS IF DESIRED
 23    IF P = 0 THEN 25
 24      GOSUB 400
 25    REMARK -- TEST FOR COMPLETION AND SELECT NEXT BET
 26      GOSUB 500
 27    REMARK -- SPIN AGAIN
 28      GO TO 15
 30    REM
100    REMARK -- SUBROUTINE TO READ DATA
101    READ C, B, U, N, P, S9
102    PRINT "TOTAL CAPITAL =", C
103    PRINT "BASIC BET =", B
104    PRINT "UPPER LIMIT =", U
105    PRINT "INITIAL SPINS =", N
106    IF P = 0 THEN 109
107      PRINT "COMPLETE RECORD REQUESTED"
108        GO TO 110
109      PRINT "ONLY FINAL RESULTS REQUESTED "
110    IF S9 = 1 THEN 113
111      PRINT "STRATEGY IS TO BET ON RED EACH TIME"
112        GO TO 114
113      PRINT "STRATEGY IS TO BET ON 1 EACH TIME"
114      PRINT
115    RETURN
117    REM
200    REMARK -- SUBROUTINE TO PERFORM INITIAL PROCESSING
201    REMARK -- MAKE INITIAL SPINS
202    FOR I = 1 TO N
203      LET Z = RND(1)
204    NEXT I
205    REMARK -- SET UP INITIAL WAGER
206    LET W = B
207    REMARK -- SET NUMBER OF SPINS TO ZERO
208    LET S = 0
209    RETURN
```

```
210   REM
250   REMARK -- SUBROUTINE TO SPIN WHEEL
251   LET R = INT( 1 + (38*RND(0)) )
252   IF R = 39 THEN 251
253   LET S = S + 1
254   RETURN
255   REM
300   REMARK -- SUBROUTINE FOR STRATEGY 0
301   IF R <= 15 THEN 306
302   REMARK -- LOST
303     LET 09 = 0
304     LET C = C - W
305     RETURN
306   REMARK -- WON
307     LET 09 = 1
308     LET C = C + W
309     RETURN
310   REM
350   REMARK -- SUBROUTINE FOR STRATEGY 1
351   IF R = 1 THEN 356
352   REMARK -- LOST
353     LET 09 = 0
354     LET C = C - W
355     RETURN
356   REMARK -- WON
357     LET 09 = 1
358     LET C = C + (35*W)
359     RETURN
360   REM
400   REMARK -- SUBROUTINE TO PRINT RESULTS OF A SPIN
401   PRINT "SPIN NUMBER", S
402   PRINT "YOU BET", W
403   PRINT "WHEEL CAME UP", R
404   PRINT "YOU NOW HAVE", C
405   PRINT
406   RETURN
407   REM
500   REMARK -- TEST FOR COMPLETION AND SELECT NEXT BET
501   IF C = 0 THEN 520
502   IF C >= U THEN 530
503   REMARK -- PLAY AGAIN
504   IF 09 = 0 THEN 510
505   REMARK -- PREVIOUS BET WON
506     LET W = B
507     GO TO 515
510   REMARK -- PREVIOUS BET LOST, DOUBLE IT
511     LET W = 2 * W
515   REMARK -- CHECK CAPITAL
516   IF C > W THEN 519
517   REMARK -- LOWER WAGER
518     LET W = C
519   RETURN
520   REMARK -- WIPED OUT
521     PRINT "SORRY -- WIPED OUT AFTER ";S;"SPINS"
522     STOP
530   REMARK -- MADE IT
531     PRINT "UPPER LIMIT REACHED AFTER";S;"SPINS"
532     PRINT "YOUR CAPITAL IS NOW", C
533     PRINT "CONGRATULATIONS"
534   STOP
```

Canned Programs

Many people who use computers do not attempt to master a programming language at all; instead, they simply rely on professional programmers who have (it is hoped) anticipated their needs when preparing programs. Certainly one need not program his own routine to do regression analysis, or linear programming, or any of a number of generally utilized techniques. It is far more efficient for a professional programmer to devote his time to preparing a general purpose, well written, and highly efficient program for such an application. Such "production," "canned," or "package" programs should meet the following criteria:

1. They should be extremely simple to use: This means that input can be prepared by simply following a few straightforward instructions.
2. They should be truly general purpose; several variations of the technique should be available with only a few alterations in input data required to obtain a different variation (unfortunately this criterion is often in conflict with the first).
3. They should provide output describing the results explicitly and requiring little or no knowledge of the underlying (solution) technique on the part of the user.
4. They should anticipate virtually any type of error that the user might make when preparing his input data; moreover, such errors should be identified on the output when detected.
5. Finally, they should be efficient (require minimal computer time) and thoroughly checked (they should work).

The language in which a program is written is of little concern to the user who wants to do exactly what the program is designed to do. But it is not unusual to find that a few changes in the program will be required if it is to serve the exact purpose the user had in mind. Under these conditions the language used is important, as is the program's documentation. Since no program can be truly general purpose, some canned programs are written as subroutines (or sets of subroutines); the user is then expected to incorporate them in a program written to serve his particular needs.

Problems

1. Write a statement to round variable Z to the nearest integer (whole number); assume that Z is positive.

2. Write a statement to round variable Z to the nearest tenth (*i.e.*, one decimal place); assume that Z is positive.
3. Assume that variable G represents gross pay in dollars. Write a statement to round it to the nearest cent.
4. Write a subroutine that will round variable A to the nearest value with N places to the right of the decimal point.
5. Write some statements to set up a list Z containing the logarithms of the first N numbers in some other list X.
6. What is the output from the following program segment?

```
  5    LET X = 0
 10    GOSUB 100
 20    PRINT 4
 30    STOP
100    PRINT 1,
110    IF X = 0 THEN 200
115    RETURN
200    PRINT 2,
202    LET X = 1
205    GOSUB 100
210    PRINT 3,
212    RETURN
```

Note in this case we have a subroutine calling itself. Will it get into an "infinite loop"? Why, or why not?

7. How would you modify the program shown on pages 76 and 77 if strategy one involved splitting the bet between numbers 1 and 2?
8. How would you modify the program shown on pages 76 and 77 to have the computer stop if play continues for a thousand spins?
9. Write a program segment that will generate fifty random integers between (and including) the values of 1 and 3. Print each as "one," "two," or "three."
10. Write a statement that assigns the following value to B7: The logarithm of the absolute value of the sine of the square root of the integer portion of Z9.

Answers

1.

```
10  LET Z = INT(Z + .5)
```

2.

```
10  LET Z = .1 * INT((10 * Z) + .5)
```

3.

```
10  LET G = .01 * INT((100 * G) + .5)
```

4.

```
100  LET P = 10 ↑ N
101  LET A = (1/P) * INT((P * A)+.5)
102  RETURN
```

5.

```
100     FOR I = 1 TO N
101       LET Z(I) = LOG(X(I))
102     NEXT I
```

6. 1 2 1 3 4

The computer will not get into an unending loop because the value of X is altered after the first pass through the subroutine. On the second pass through, it is tested to see if the value has been changed. Upon finding out it has been, the computer promptly returns to the place from which it came via the GOSUB.

7. Alter the print statement:

```
113  PRINT "STRATEGY IS TO BET 1 AND 2 EACH TIME"
```

Alter the subroutine for strategy one:

```
351  IF R < = 2 THEN 356
 •
 •
 •
358  LET C = C + (35 * (W/2))
```

8. The solution is to check S each time. This can be done in any of a number of places in the program. For example:

```
26    GOSUB 500
27    IF S > 1000 THEN 30
28    REMARK -- SPIN AGAIN
29      GO TO 15
30    REMARK -- TOO MANY SPINS
31      GOSUB 400
32      STOP
```

Notice that you need not write a special set of statements to indicate the player's situation at this point; just GOSUB 400. This output would be particularly helpful if the user had not requested output after each spin.

9. One solution is:

```
10    FOR L = 1 TO 50
12      LET R = INT(1 + RND(0)*3)
14      IF R = 4 THEN 12
16      IF R > 1 THEN 22
18      PRINT "ONE"
20      GO TO 35
22      IF R > 2 THEN 28
24      PRINT "TWO"
26      GO TO 35
28      PRINT "THREE"
35    NEXT L
```

10.

```
LET B7 = LOG(ABS(SIN(SQR(INT(Z9)))))
```

Chapter 8

Conversational Programming

In previous chapters we saw how the computer utilizes a BASIC program to operate on data. We always gave it data in the form of numbers included in DATA statements and then used READ statements to store the numbers in mailboxes so that other instructions could process them.

This method of supplying the computer with data requires that all the numbers be specified before the program is executed. Sometimes it may not be convenient, or even possible, to do so. For example, you might wish to see some of the program's results before selecting certain values to be input. You can do this by using the INPUT command to give the computer data during the execution of the program.

The INPUT Command

The READ command was an instruction to: "Take the number from the top of the data stack and store it in the mailbox indicated." The INPUT command also stores data items in mailboxes; but instead of taking the items from the data stack, it causes the computer to wait for you to type them in from your console. To see how it works, look at the following command:

```
100   INPUT Z6
```

When the computer encounters it, three things happen:

1. A character, usually a question mark ("?") is printed on the output sheet. This lets you know that the computer wants a data item.

2. Execution of the program is stopped until you are through. When you are, you signal the computer. In most systems the appropriate signal is a carriage return.
3. The number the computer receives from you is stored in variable Z6, and execution proceeds to the statement following line 100.

Thus when line 100 is reached, a question mark will appear on the output sheet:

?

You respond by typing a number:

? 53.57

The computer will wait for your signal and upon receiving it will store the number, 53.57, in variable Z6 before continuing execution.

You may use input statements to enter data for any variable you wish. And you may enter data for more than one variable at a time. For example, the command:

INPUT Q4, S(3), W(N + 5,7)

will cause a question mark to be printed as before. But this time the computer will expect you to give it three numbers, separated by commas, before signaling it that you are done. Thus when the question mark appears, you might respond in the following way:

? 29.5, 67, 45.98

Just as with a DATA statement, the numbers are assigned to variables in the order that they appear from left to right. In this case 29.5 will be assigned to Q4, 67 will be assigned to S(3), and 45.98 will be assigned to W(N + 5, 7).

Suppose you want to get some numbers from the data stack and others from the console. No problem. Because input statements do not interfere with the data stack, you are free to continue using READ and DATA statements just as before. Whenever you want a number from the stack, just use READ; whenever you want one from the console, use INPUT.

Using Print Statements with INPUT

It is helpful to include a PRINT statement before each INPUT statement in your program. Then you won't have to remember the order in which the program requires numbers; just let the PRINT statement refresh your memory. Here is an example:

```
50    PRINT "WHAT IS YOUR AGE ";
51    INPUT A
60    PRINT "AND YOUR WEIGHT ";
61    INPUT W
```

The output, after one person responded, looked like this:

```
WHAT IS YOUR AGE ? 21
AND YOUR WEIGHT ? 115
```

After line 50 was executed, the output was:

WHAT IS YOUR AGE

Upon reaching line 51, the computer printed a question mark:

WHAT IS YOUR AGE ?

The response, 21, was typed in by the person:

WHAT IS YOUR AGE ? 21

After storing the number in variable A, the computer proceeded to line 60. And so on.

But something strange happened when line 60 was encountered. The printing once again started at the left margin of a new line even though a dangling semicolon had been used in line 50. Why? In systems where the user signals the computer with a carriage return after typing his numbers, the computer will resume at the left margin automatically.

One of the advantages of printing strings before input commands is that others can use your program with a minimum of prior study. Suppose you wanted to write a security analysis program to be used by a businessman who didn't know anything about programming. You might start it in the following way:

```
10    REMARK -- SECURITY ANALYSIS PROGRAM
15    REMARK -- INPUT DATA
20    PRINT "HOW MANY SECURITIES DO YOU HAVE ";
21    INPUT N
30    PRINT "HOW MANY MONTHLY PRICES FOR EACH ";
31    INPUT M
40    PRINT
50    FOR I = 1 TO N
51      FOR J = 1 TO M
52        PRINT "PRICE FOR SEC. ";I;"MONTH ";J;
53        INPUT S(I,J)
55      NEXT J
57    NEXT I
```

Notice that the strings provide all the information the businessman will need in order to have his securities analyzed. He won't need to know anything about your program, nor will he have to bother learning to write DATA statements.

Here's what the output might look like for a case involving two securities:

```
HOW MANY SECURITIES DO YOU HAVE ? 2
HOW MANY MONTHLY PRICES FOR EACH ? 2

PRICE FOR SEC.  1     MONTH  1     ? 50.25
PRICE FOR SEC.  1     MONTH  2     ? 52.75
PRICE FOR SEC.  2     MONTH  1     ? 34.50
PRICE FOR SEC.  2     MONTH  2     ? 30.00
```

This approach is also useful if you wish to have more than one number input at a time. Consider the following program segment:

```
100  PRINT "GIVE ME 2 NUMBERS—AGE,WEIGHT ";
101  INPUT A, W
```

Without line 100 you might forget that two numbers are required. If the wrong number of items is typed, various things can happen (depending on the system). If too few numbers are given, the computer will usually respond with another question mark. If too many are given, the computer may save the extra numbers to use the next time it needs an item from the console. Rather than trying to guess what will happen if you input the wrong number of items, it is a good idea to use print statements like this to increase the chances that the exact number will be input.

An Application

Input commands enable you (or someone else) to decide on certain data values after seeing some of your program's preliminary results. This allows the user to carry on a "conversation" with your program. For example, the data values input can be used within the program as the basis for decisions. Suppose you want the user to be able to decide, at line 18, whether to go next to line 100 or to line 200. Just say:

```
18  INPUT R
19  IF R = 0 THEN 100
20  GO TO 200
```

There are many occasions when decisions of this sort are useful. The game of blackjack provides an illustration.

Blackjack is played with an ordinary deck of cards. Each card in the deck is worth a certain number of points: Numbered cards are worth their face values; jacks, queens, and kings are worth ten; aces are worth either one or eleven. Any number of players may play against the "house"; the object is to obtain cards totaling less than twenty-two but more than the dealer has. Cards are dealt to a player one at a time until he decides to "stand pat." If at that time his cards total more than twenty-one, he automatically loses.

At each stage of the game a player's decision either to draw another card or to stand pat should be based on the cards he already holds. Therefore, he would like to know the last card drawn before making each decision.

How might a computer program be written to play blackjack? Let's say you want to play against the computer (who is also the dealer). (For purposes of illustration, we shall use rules slightly simpler than those employed by Las Vegas casinos.) First, the program should instruct the computer to set up the deck, shuffle it, and deal itself a card face up. Then it should deal you two cards. After telling you (*i.e.*, printing) what your cards were, the computer should ask you (with an input command, of course) if you want another card. We will let a non-zero number indicate you want another; if you give the computer a "0" it will assume you wish to stand pat. Of course, the decisions about cards dealt to the dealer can be made without the further use of the input command.

A program to play blackjack follows. Lines 10 through 25 print the rules of play. In lines 30 through 37 the total points for the dealer and the player are initialized to zero. Then the computer goes to subroutine 200 (in line 39) which sets up the "deck": list D containing 52 items numbered from 1 through 13. In lines 40 through 47, the computer draws a card for itself and prints the results. Subroutine 300, however, actually does the drawing. How? By picking a random number between 1 and the number of cards left in the deck (in this case, 52). The number drawn determines which item in list D is to be used. Subroutine 400 prints the results of the drawings and keeps a running total of the points for both dealer and player.

Your turn comes in lines 50 through 74. The computer deals you two cards (lines 52 through 57); then it asks you if you want another. When you decide to stand pat, the computer will print your best score (valuing aces at either one or eleven) in line 73. If your score is over twenty-one, you lose (line 75).

The dealer's strategy for deciding whether to draw again (if you aren't over twenty-one) is given in line 91. He will always stand pat if his total points (valuing aces at eleven) exceed sixteen. If you wish to try some alternative strategy for him, this is the instruction you should modify.

The dealer continues to deal himself cards (lines 83 through 86) until he is ready to stand pat. After printing out the dealer's total points (line 102), the computer will determine the winner (lines 150 through 170) and ask you if you care to play again (lines 181 through 185).

```
10    REMARK -- BLACKJACK GAME
11    REM
12    REMARK -- PRINT INSTRUCTIONS TO PLAYER
13    PRINT "THIS IS A GAME OF BLACKJACK.  YOU WILL"
14    PRINT "BE PLAYING AGAINST THE HOUSE.  EACH TIME"
15    PRINT "THE DEALER ASKS YOU IF YOU WANT ANOTHER"
16    PRINT "CARD, PLEASE RESPOND WITH A 1 IF YOU DO,"
17    PRINT "0 IF YOU DO NOT."
18    PRINT "THE RULES ARE AS FOLLOWS:"
19    PRINT "  1.  EACH CARD HAS POINTS EQUAL TO ITS FACE"
20    PRINT "      VALUE.  JACKS, QUEENS, KINGS = 10."
21    PRINT "      ACES MAY EQUAL 1 OR 11."
22    PRINT "  2.  YOU WIN IF YOUR POINTS TOTAL"
23    PRINT "      MORE THAN THE HOUSE BUT <= 21."
24    PRINT "  3.  INITIALLY, YOU MAY SEE ONE CARD DRAWN"
25    PRINT "      BY THE HOUSE."
26    PRINT
28    REM
30    REMARK -- INITIALIZE
31    DIM D(52),F(2),R(2,2)
32    FOR I = 1 TO 2
34      FOR J = 1 TO 2
35        LET R(I,J) = 0
36      NEXT J
37    NEXT I
38    REMARK -- SET UP DECK
39    GOSUB 200
40    REMARK -- DEAL A CARD TO HOUSE. P=1
43    LET P = 1
45    GOSUB 300
46    PRINT "HOUSE CARD IS A";
47    GOSUB 400
48    PRINT
50    REMARK -- DEAL TWO CARDS TO PLAYER. P = 2
51    LET P = 2
52    FOR I = 1 TO 2
54      GOSUB 300
55      PRINT "YOUR CARD IS A";
56      GOSUB 400
57    NEXT I
60    PRINT
61    PRINT "DO YOU WANT ANOTHER CARD ";
62    INPUT A
63    IF A = 0 THEN 70
64    GOSUB 300
65    PRINT "YOUR NEXT CARD IS A";
67    GOSUB 400
68    GO TO 60
70    REMARK -- PLAYER QUITS.  COMPUTE FINAL SCORE
71    GOSUB 500
73    PRINT "YOU STAND PAT.  TOTAL POINTS = "; F(P)
74    PRINT
```

```
 75   IF F(P) > 21 THEN 170
 80   REMARK -- HOUSE DRAWS AGAIN
 81   REMARK -- STRATEGY FOR HOUSE:
 82   REMARK -- STAND PAT AT 17. (ACES = 11)
 83   LET P = 1
 84   GOSUB 300
 85   PRINT "NEXT HOUSE CARD IS A";
 86   GOSUB 400
 90   REMARK -- CHECK POINTS SO FAR
 91   IF R(P,2) < 17 THEN 84
100   REMARK -- HOUSE STANDS PAT.  COMPUTE FINAL SCORE
101   GOSUB 500
102   PRINT "HOUSE STANDS PAT.  TOTAL POINTS = ";F(P)
103   REM
150   REMARK -- DETERMINE WINNER
153   IF F(1) = 21 THEN 170
154   IF F(1) > 21 THEN 160
155   IF F(1) >= F(2) THEN 170
160   PRINT "CONGRATULATIONS.  YOU JUST WON."
161   GO TO 180
170   PRINT "SORRY, THE HOUSE WON."
180   PRINT
181   PRINT "IF YOU WOULD LIKE TO PLAY AGAIN,"
182   PRINT "INPUT A 1.  IF NOT, INPUT A 0 ";
183   INPUT Z
184   PRINT
185   IF Z = 1 THEN 30
186   STOP
187   REM
200   REMARK -- CREATE DECK OF CARDS
202   REMARK -- LIST D CONTAINS FACE VALUE OF EACH CARD
204   REMARK -- N IS INITIALIZED TO 52: THE NUMBER OF
205   REMARK -- CARDS IN THE DECK.
206   LET N9 = 0
210   FOR I = 1 TO 4
211     FOR J = 1 TO 13
212       LET N9 = N9 + 1
213       LET D(N9) = J
214     NEXT J
215   NEXT I
216   LET N = 52
217   RETURN
218   REM
300   REMARK -- DRAW A CARD
301   REMARK -- C IS THE CARD DRAWN
302   REMARK -- N IS THE NUMBER OF UNDRAWN CARDS IN DECK
303   LET K = INT(1 + (RND(0) * N))
304   LET C = D(K)
305   LET D(K) = D(N)
306   LET N = N - 1
307   RETURN
310   REM
400   REMARK -- PRINT VALUE OF CARD DRAWN AND ADD TO
401   REMARK -- TOTAL POINTS.
402   REMARK -- R(P,1) IS POINTS WITH ACES = 1
403   REMARK -- R(P,2) IS POINTS WITH ACES = 11
404   IF C > 10 THEN 415
405   LET R(P,1) = R(P,1) + C
406   IF C = 1 THEN 410
407   LET R(P,2) = R(P,2) + C
408   PRINT C
409   RETURN
410   PRINT "N ACE"
411   LET R(P,2) = R(P,2) + 11
412   RETURN
415   IF C > 11 THEN 420
416   PRINT " JACK"
```

```
417    GO TO 426
420    IF C > 12 THEN 425
421    PRINT " QUEEN"
422    GO TO 426
425    PRINT " KING"
426    LET R(P,1) = R(P,1) + 10
427    LET R(P,2) = R(P,2) + 10
429    RETURN
430    REM
500    REMARK -- COMPUTE FINAL SCORE: F(P)
501    IF R(P,1) = R(P,2) THEN 510
502    IF R(P,2) > 21 THEN 510
503    LET F(P) = R(P,2)
505    RETURN
510    LET F(P) = R(P,1)
511    RETURN
```

Problems

1. What, if anything, is wrong with the following responses to input commands? Assume that in every case the program wants one number.
   (a) HOW MANY CHILDREN DO YOU HAVE ? I HAVE 3.
   (b) WHAT IS YOUR ANNUAL INCOME ? 7,000
   (c) HOW MANY INCHES IN A FOOT ? 25.30
   (d) A PINT IS WHAT PORTION OF A QUART ? 1/2
2. When the input command is used, it is a good idea to check for errors the user might make in input values. Write a program segment that asks the user for a perfect square (*i.e.*, a number whose square root is a whole number) and then asks him to try again if he gave you a number that wasn't a perfect square.
3. Assume you work for a small market research firm. You have been asked to interview local citizens regarding their television viewing habits. Among the questions you must ask each interviewee are the following:
   a. Do you own a television?
   b. If not, do you contemplate buying one in the next year?
   c. If yes, do you watch it during the daytime
      (1) often
      (2) seldom
      (3) never

   Write a program to ask these questions.
4. Write a program that checks for "lucky numbers" in a supermarket drawing. The supermarket in question has issued tickets numbered 1 through 1000. Using the input command, ask for a ticketholder's number; then check to see if it is "lucky." Numbers whose last two digits are "17" win $10; numbers divisible by 30 win $5. Print the winnings, if any.

Answers

1. (a) "I HAVE 3" is not a number.
   (b) The user gave the program too many numbers.
   (c) This is perfectly acceptable. The computer looks only to see if the number is a legal constant.
   (d) 1/2 is an expression, not a legal constant. Expressions may not be used as data items, either in data statements or as responses to input commands. The user should have typed the fraction in decimal form: *e.g.*, as 0.5.
2. Here is one way you might write it:

```
50   PRINT "GIVE ME A NUMBER THAT IS A PERFECT SQUARE ";
51   INPUT S
52   IF S < 0 THEN 70
53   IF SQR(S) = INT(SQR(S)) THEN 80
60   PRINT "TRY AGAIN.";S;"IS NOT A PERFECT SQUARE. "
61   PRINT "WHAT IS YOUR NEXT CHOICE ";
62   GO TO 51
70   PRINT "SORRY, BUT";S;"IS NEGATIVE.  TRY AGAIN. "
72   GO TO 61
80   PRINT "VERY GOOD."
81   REMARK -- PROCEED
```

3. Your program might look something like this:

```
10   REMARK -- INTERVIEWING PROGRAM: TELEVISION
11   REMARK -- VIEWING HABITS
13   DIM A(3)
15   PRINT "HELLO.  I WOULD LIKE TO ASK YOU SOME"
16   PRINT "QUESTIONS ABOUT YOUR T.V. VIEWING."
17   PRINT
18   PRINT "IF YOU OWN A TELEVISION, PLEASE TYPE"
19   PRINT "A 1.  IF YOU DONT, TYPE 0 ";
20   INPUT A(1)
30   IF A(1) = 1 THEN 50
40   PRINT "IF YOU PLAN TO BUY ONE IN THE NEXT YEAR"
41   PRINT "TYPE A 1.  IF NOT, TYPE 0 ";
42   INPUT A(2)
43   GO TO 60
50   PRINT "DO YOU WATCH YOUR TELEVISION DURING THE"
51   PRINT "DAYTIME:"
52   PRINT "  1  OFTEN"
53   PRINT "  2  SELDOM"
54   PRINT "  3  NEVER"
55   PRINT "TYPE A 1, 2, OR 3 ";
56   INPUT A(3)
60   PRINT
62   PRINT "THANK YOU."
63   STOP
```

4. One answer might be:

```
  1   REMARK -- SUPERMARKET DRAWING
  5   PRINT "WHAT IS YOUR NUMBER ";
  7   INPUT N
 10   IF N < 1 THEN 40
 11   IF N > 1000 THEN 40
 12   IF (N-17)/100 <> INT((N-17)/100) THEN 20
 13   PRINT "CONGRATULATIONS! YOU WON $10."
 14   STOP
 20   IF N/30 <> INT(N/30) THEN 30
 21   PRINT "NOT BAD.  YOU WON $5."
 22   STOP
 30   PRINT "SORRY, YOU DIDNT WIN THIS TIME."
 31   STOP
 40   REMARK -- HE MADE A MISTAKE
 41   PRINT "TAKE ANOTHER LOOK AT YOUR NUMBER."
 42   PRINT "WHAT IS IT ";
 43   GO TO 7
```

Note: If you don't believe line 12 works, try it yourself. By subtracting 17 from any positive number ending in the digits "17", you will get either an even multiple of 100 or 0. But 0/100 is itself a whole number (*i.e.*, 0).

Part II

Extended BASIC

Introduction to Part II

If you have studied Part I carefully and tried to run your own programs on a computer, you should feel reasonably comfortable with the BASIC language. You can write programs to process virtually any numeric data and print the results in a fairly attractive manner. If you go no farther in this book, you can still be confident that your knowledge of BASIC will allow you to solve a good many interesting problems quickly and efficiently.

Only a few of the features described in Part II enable you to do something you cannot do with essential BASIC; most of them allow you to take shortcuts, however. And if you plan to use a computer quite a bit, you will find these shortcuts invaluable. Some, such as matrix commands, are tailor-made for particular kinds of problems. Others will be useful in diverse situations. And some features (such as string variables and certain printing features) will allow you to do new things.

A word of caution is in order at this point. BASIC is available on many computer systems. Essential BASIC—described in Part I—can be used "as is" on almost all of them. This is not true of extended BASIC. Although we deal primarily with features common to a majority of systems, be forewarned that a particular feature may not be available on the system you are using (or it may be available, but in a slightly different form). Before using a specific computer, it would be wise to check the official manual for the system to get the specifications of the particular version of BASIC it understands.

Chapter 9

More on Strings

Chapter 4 showed how to print messages with strings. Although this is useful, many applications also require the ability to read strings as data and to process them as well.

String Variables

Earlier, a string was defined as a sequence of characters enclosed in quotation marks. For example:

"WINNIE-THE-POOH"
"*$/+(−)"

In many BASIC systems special mailboxes have been set aside to hold strings (just as the mailboxes previously discussed were set aside to hold numbers). These new mailboxes are called, logically, *string variables*. There are twenty-six of them. Each is named with a letter followed by a dollar sign: A$, B$, . . . , Z$.

Use of Strings with LET and PRINT

A string variable may be assigned a value in a LET statement. Examples are:

```
LET Z$ = "YES"
LET R$ = A$
```

The first command assigns the three-character string "YES" to Z$. The second assigns a copy of the string in A$ to R$.

The string assigned to a string variable may contain any characters except embedded quotation marks. The following is perfectly legal:

```
LET W$ = "123.65"
```

However, W$ will contain the six characters "123.65", *not* the numeric value 123.65. String variables should not be used to hold numbers; thus in most systems it is illegal to say:

```
LET W$ = 123.65
```

Although the distinction between the string "123.65" and the number 123.65 may seem unclear to you now, its importance will soon be evident.

There is always a restriction on the maximum number of characters you may store in a string variable, since computer mailboxes are limited in size. Almost all systems can store fifteen-character strings (counting any blanks, but not quotation marks); many can handle considerably longer ones. If, for some reason, you try to store a string that is longer than the maximum allowed, the right end is likely to be chopped off.

String variables may be printed:

```
PRINT S$
PRINT Y$; A$
PRINT A, 47.5, "HELLO"; F$
```

The comma works the way it always has, and the semicolon gives you the same spacing as if the strings had been written explicitly. Thus if A$ = "DATE—" and B$ = "DEC. 25, 1969", then:

```
PRINT A$;B$
```

would produce the output:

```
DATE—DEC. 25, 1969
```

As always, the quotation marks are not printed.

Reading and Inputting Strings

If you wish to read a string as data, just say:

```
READ A$
```

The corresponding data statement might look like this:

```
DATA "JOHN JONES"
```

More than one string may be read at a time, and string variables may be intermixed with numeric variables in READ and DATA statements. Consider, for example, the following revision of the payroll program:

```
 5   PRINT "NAME", "PAY RATE", "GROSS PAY",
 7   PRINT "WITHHOLDING", "NET"
10   READ N$,P,H
20   PRINT N$, P, H, .14*(P*H), .86*(P*H)
30   GO TO 10
```

One set of data for it is shown below:

```
900   REM--DATA FOR PAYROLL PROGRAM
901   DATA "JANE ADAMS", 2.25, 40
902   DATA "BOB CARTER", 3.00, 41
903   DATA "JOHN JONES", 2.97, 35
904   DATA "SAM MILLER", 3.10, 49
```

The rules the computer follows for ordering items in the data stack are the same as before. Just be sure to place the items in DATA statements so that strings will be read into string variables and numbers will be read into numeric variables.

Inputting strings is equally easy. Some examples of legal input statements and appropriate responses follow:

Statement	*Response*
INPUT C$	? "COLUMBUS"
INPUT E$, A1	? "SALES", 250
INPUT R(1), W$, Q$, P(N*K,S)	? 35, "YES", "NO", 2.4

Not surprisingly, commas are used as separators between strings and numbers in responses.

Comparing Strings

Strings may be compared using IF statements. All six of the comparisons introduced in Chapter 3 are legal. For example, the statement:

IF A$ = "YES" THEN 100

causes the computer to transfer to line 100 if the string currently stored in A$ matches the string "YES".

The contents of two string variables might be compared by saying:

```
IF G$ <> H$ THEN 450
```

Two strings are "unequal" if they are not *exact* copies of each other. Thus, "123.65" and "123.650" are not equal; neither are " SMITH" and "SMITH". (Remember blanks are important in strings.)

Other valid comparisons are:

```
IF W$ <  Z$ THEN 300
IF Q$ >  "ADAMS" THEN 260
IF A$ < = B$ THEN 10
IF "JONES" > = "JOHNSON" THEN 635
```

But what does it mean to ask if one string is "greater than" or "less than or equal to" another?

The computer has ranked all the characters it recognizes in order from "lowest" to "highest." When a comparison between two strings is made, the computer proceeds in the following way: It compares the first character of one string with the first character of the other. If the two characters are the same, it compares the second characters of both, then the third, and so on. When it finds a character in the first string that is not equal to the corresponding one in the other, that character becomes the basis for the decision. If it is of lower rank than its counterpart in the second string, the first string is "less than" the second. If it is of higher rank, the first string is the "greater" of the two. And if the computer runs out of characters in one string before finding any mismatches, the shorter string is the "lesser."

The procedure is just like the one lexicographers use to order the words in a dictionary. Hence, we can think of strings as having some sort of *lexicographic ordering* which IF statements can interrogate for us. We might want to know if "1A" comes before "2A" in the computer's "dictionary," for example. Or if the string currently in F$ comes before the one in E$.

Obviously, in order to know how the computer orders strings in its dictionary, it is necessary to know how it ranks individual characters. Two ranking rules are:

1. Letters (A to Z) are ranked in alphabetic order.
2. Digits (0 to 9) are ranked in numeric order.

This is just what you'd want it to do. "JOHNSON" comes before "JONES"; "1A" comes before "2A"; "676" comes before "677", and so on. And because ties are broken on the basis of length, "SAM" comes before "SAMUEL" and "15" comes before "150".

Comparisons between a letter and a digit, a digit and a special symbol (such as *,/,$,%), or a special symbol and a letter should be undertaken with great care. In many systems all letters are ranked higher than digits; in others, however, the reverse may be true. Thus one system may rank "B5" greater than "5B"; another may not. Moral: Avoid making such comparisons unless you know your computer's rankings.

It is important to remember that although strings may contain digits, they have no numeric value. Even though the string "123" may be "less than" the string "1234", comparisons between a string and a numeric constant are meaningless (as well as illegal). Strings can be compared only with other strings, and numbers compared only with other numbers.

String Lists

Strings may be put into lists, too. Legal list names are the same as for simple string variables: A$, B$, . . . , and so on, through Z$. If you want to read ten strings into list R$, you can do so by saying:

```
10   FOR I = 1 TO 10
20     READ R$(I)
30   NEXT I
```

After execution of this program, each element in R$ will contain a single string. The INPUT command may also be used to "fill" string lists.

As before, if you anticipate putting more than ten items in a list, you must reserve space in a DIM statement. Numeric lists and tables may be included in the same DIM statement. It is legal to say:

DIM T$(20), P(30,10), W(11), S$(4)

The CHANGE Statement

Some systems have special features that allow you to take strings apart and create new ones, look for the occurrence of particular characters in a string, or find the length of a string.

One such feature is the CHANGE statement. It changes a string variable into a numeric list by substituting "code numbers" for each of the characters in the string. Suppose, for example, that V$ = "HELLO". Then the instruction:

CHANGE V$ TO V

causes a list V to be created whose elements are code numbers representing the letters, H, E, L, L, O. The zero-th item in V will contain a number equal to the number of characters in V$.[1] Assume the codes for the letters in V$ are those given below:

Letter	*Code*
E	69
H	72
L	76
O	79

After the CHANGE statement has been executed, list V will look like this:

V(0) = 5
V(1) = 72
V(2) = 69
V(3) = 76
V(4) = 76
V(5) = 79

The code for the first character of V$ is in V(1), the code for the second character is in V(2), and so on. V(0) contains the length, 5, of V$.

The process can be reversed, too. The instruction:

CHANGE V TO V$

creates the string "HELLO" from the code numbers in V and stores it in V$. The zero-th item in V tells the computer how many code numbers should be changed back into characters.

The CHANGE statement can be used in various ways. Assume you wish to create a new string from two others stored in A$ and B$. At the present time, A$ = "BLACK" and B$ = "JACK"; the new string you want is "BLACKJACK". Here is a program to create it:

```
50    CHANGE A$ TO X
52    CHANGE B$ TO Y
53    LET L1 = X(0)
55    FOR I = 1 TO Y(0)
57       LET L1 = L1 + 1
58       LET X(L1) = Y(I)
60    NEXT I
65    LET X(0) = X(0) + Y(0)
67    CHANGE X TO C$
70    PRINT "THE RESULTING STRING IS "; C$
71    STOP
```

1. The CHANGE statement is available only in systems that allow lists to have zero-th items.

Lines 50 and 52 change A$ and B$ into lists of code numbers; the code numbers for A$ are stored in list X, and the code numbers for B$ are stored in list Y. Since the contents of X(0) tell us A$'s length, it is a simple matter to move the items in Y into list X, starting with the first "empty" item in X. And there are Y(0) items to move. After all the items in Y have been transferred to X, the only job remaining is to update X(0). Because we wish to create a new string containing the characters in A$ followed by the characters in B$, the length should equal X(0) + Y(0). Therefore, line 65 assigns the value (X(0) + Y(0)) to X(0). The desired result is obtained by changing list X into string C$.

Remember that the code numbers are numeric values; therefore, they may be manipulated like any other number. For example, if you want to ask whether the third character in V$ is an "L", you could say:

```
IF V(3) = 76 THEN 100
```

String Functions

Some systems provide certain *string functions* that make the CHANGE statement unnecessary.

The LENGTH function yields a number equal to the length of the string given as an argument—*i.e.*, inside the parentheses. For example:

```
LENGTH(A$)
```

In some systems the function is named LEN; thus you might be required to say LEN(A$). In any event the outcome is simple enough: The characters in the specific string are counted and the resulting number substituted. If A$ = "5 DOLLARS" then LENGTH(A$) = 9. Recall that blanks are important in strings, so they are included in the character count.

You may use the LENGTH function wherever an arithmetic expression is legal. For example:

```
LET A3 = LENGTH(A$)
PRINT LENGTH(B$)
IF LENGTH(R$) > = LENGTH(W$) THEN 100
FOR I = 1 TO LENGTH(C$) STEP 2
```

Another useful function is INDEX. It has the following form:

INDEX(*string*, *string*)

Either argument may be a string variable or an explicit string (for example, "ABC").

Like the LENGTH function, INDEX also yields a number. If the second string in the argument is part of the first, the value of the function is the position in the first string at which the second string starts. If the second string is not part of the first, the value of the function is zero. For example, INDEX("ABC", "B") = 2. If A$ = "1543" and B$ = "75", then INDEX(A$, B$) = 0.

If the INDEX function yields a non-zero value, we say that the second string is a *substring* of the first. Thus, "JOHN" is a substring of "JOHNSON". But "JHSN" is not; a substring must represent consecutive characters. It also might occur more than once, as "O" does in "JOHNSON". If it does, INDEX will give you the position of the first occurrence. Since "O" occurs first as the second character, INDEX("JOHNSON", "O") will equal 2.

Here is a sample program segment using INDEX:

```
300    LET C$ = "COLUMBUS"
310    PRINT "WHO DISCOVERED AMERICA ";
315    INPUT N$
320    IF INDEX(N$,C$) = 1 THEN 400
325    REM -- THERE'S STILL HOPE
330    IF INDEX(N$,"UMBUS") = 4 THEN 420
335    REM -- TRY ONCE MORE
340    IF INDEX(N$,"C") = 1 THEN 440
345    PRINT "TRY AGAIN.  HIS NAME BEGINS WITH C."
350    PRINT "WHO WAS HE ";
355    GO TO 315
400    REM -- HE GOT IT RIGHT
410    PRINT "VERY GOOD."
415    GO TO 500
420    REM -- HE WAS CLOSE
425    PRINT "THATS CLOSE.  ITS COLUMBUS."
430    GO TO 500
440    REM -- HE HAS THE RIGHT FIRST LETTER ANYWAY
445    PRINT "NOT QUITE, BUT THE FIRST LETTER IS"
450    PRINT "CORRECT AT LEAST.  TRY AGAIN."
455    GO TO 350
500    REM -- CONTINUE
```

In this case INDEX was used to analyze a student's answer to the question: "Who discovered America?".

The SUBSTR(for substring) function is also extremely handy. With it you can create a new string that is a piece of an old one. It comes in two forms:

SUBSTR(*string, expression*)

and

SUBSTR(*string, expression, expression*)

The string given as the first argument may be either a string variable or an explicit string. Any expression or numeric-valued function may be used for the second or third argument.

What does SUBSTR do? It creates substrings from existing strings. For example:

LET B$ = SUBSTR(A$, 5)

This statement causes all the characters in A$ starting with the fifth one to be stored in B$. The first argument indicates the string from which a substring is to be created; the second tells which character of the original string is to be the first character of the substring.

Obviously, the SUBSTR function does not have a numeric value; it has a string value. SUBSTR("WILLIAM", 5) is equal to "IAM". And if A$ is equal to "HELLO", SUBSTR(A$, INDEX(A$, "L")) is equal to "LLO".

The second form of SUBSTR allows you to create a substring from the middle of an existing string. For example, the statement:

LET C$ = SUBSTR("ABCDEF", 3, 2)

is an instruction to: "Store in C$ a substring of "ABCDEF" which starts with the third character of the latter and has a length of 2." The third argument, if used, tells the computer how many characters the substring must have. In this case the string "CD" will be created.

There are many uses for SUBSTR. Here is a program segment to print a string with all its blanks removed:

```
10    FOR I = 1 TO LENGTH(S$)
20      LET T$ = SUBSTR(S$, I, 1)
30      IF T$ = " " THEN 50
40      PRINT T$;
50    NEXT I
```

As another example, suppose you wish to have the user of your program input a string representing a date (such as "MAY 12, 1975"). Your goal is to obtain a substring containing only the day of the month (in this case, "12"). Here is one possibility:

```
100   PRINT "GIVE ME A DATE IN THE FORM:  MAY 12, 1975 ";
115   INPUT M$
120   LET C1 = INDEX(M$, " ")
125   LET C2 = INDEX(M$, ",") - C1 - 1
130   LET D$ = SUBSTR(M$, C1 + 1, C2)
135   PRINT "THE DAY OF THE MONTH IS ";D$
140   STOP
```

Notice that the program assumes that everything after the first blank and before the comma is the day of the month. This means that the program would misbehave if the user input something like "   JANUARY 2, 1975" or "JULY30,1984". A more foolproof approach would be to scan the input string until the first digit is found; everything between it and the comma could then be treated as the day. A digit might be found by comparing each character to the strings "1", "2", and so on.

Two additional functions permit you to convert numbers to strings and strings to numbers.

The STR function converts a number to a string containing the same digits. Its standard form is:

STR(*expression*)

For example, STR(354) = "354", STR(5) = "5", and if J = 6, STR (J + 1) = "7". If the number contains a decimal point, so will the string: STR(12.5) = "12.5".

The VAL function does just the opposite: It converts a string of digits into a number. The string may be a string variable or an explicit string. The standard form is:

VAL(*string*)

For example, VAL ("85") = 85, VAL("78.95") = 78.95, and if J$ = "15.8", VAL(J$) = 15.8. Just be careful not to use a string containing a non-numeric character with the VAL function—it would make no sense, and the computer would probably tell you so.

String Addition

Sometime you may want to append some characters to the end of an existing string. On many systems this is very simple. For example, to add the characters "ABC" to the right end of the string in C$, merely say:

LET C$ = C$ + "ABC"

The plus sign does not indicate normal addition; it is a notice to link two strings together. The procedure may be used to link several strings. For example:

LET R$ = "567" + S$ + SUBSTR(T$,3) + STR(A)

If the result is too long, of course, you may lose the rightmost characters.

Conclusion

We have described some of the more useful string features available in BASIC systems. The first part of the chapter applies to virtually all systems having string variables, but some of these systems lack the CHANGE statement, string functions, and/or string addition. It might be wise to consult the reference manual for your specific system before writing a program using the features described here.

Problems

1. What is wrong with the following program (other than the fact that it is obviously nonsense)?

```
10    DIM M$(100)
15    LET A$ = "123"
20    INPUT M$
25    LET B$ = 456
30    FOR I = 1 TO 100
35      FOR J = 0 TO 9
40        IF M$(I) = STR(J) THEN 60
45      NEXT J
47    NEXT I
50    PRINT M$; "CONTAINS NO DIGITS
53    STOP
60    LET C$ = VAL(A$)
62    LET D$ = STR(VAL(A$)/VAL(B$))
65    PRINT SUBSTR(A$,1,LENGTH(A$))
70    STOP
```

2. Write a program that alphabetizes words in a dictionary. Use a string list.
3. Using the CHANGE statement, write a subroutine that performs the INDEX function. Assume the string you are working with is in A$ and the substring you want to find is in B$.
4. A word is a *palindrome* if it is spelled the same backward and forward. Examples are: radar, level, pop. Using string functions, find out if the string currently in S$ is a palindrome.
5. A *binary search* procedure can be a very quick and efficient way to search a large alphabetical dictionary. Make up a list of at least ten words in alphabetical order. Then play computer and look for a particular word in it using the following program. How does a binary search work?

```
10   PRINT "HOW MANY WORDS IN YOUR DICTIONARY ";
12   INPUT N
15   REM -- READ DICTIONARY
17   FOR I = 1 TO N
19     INPUT S$(I)
20   NEXT I
21   LET R1 = 1
22   LET R2 = N
23   LET R3 = 0
25   PRINT "WHAT IS YOUR WORD ";
30   INPUT T$
32   LET R4 = INT((R1 + R2)/2 + .5)
33   IF R4 = R3 THEN 80
34   LET R3 = R4
40   IF S$(R3) = T$ THEN 70
43   IF S$(R3) > T$ THEN 60
50   REM -- NOT FAR ENOUGH IN LIST
53   LET R1 = R3
55   GO TO 32
60   REM -- TOO FAR DOWN
62   LET R2 = R3
64   GO TO 32
70   REM -- STRING FOUND
75   PRINT "YOUR WORD IS IN THE DICTIONARY."
77   GO TO 21
80   REM -- IT MAY NOT BE HERE
82   IF S$(R3 - 1) = T$ THEN 70
83   PRINT "SORRY, ITS NOT HERE."
85   GO TO 21
```

6. You have just been hired by a corporation to think up names for its many new products. The president has given you the following rule: All proposed names must have five letters, begin with a consonant, and be composed of alternating consonants and vowels. Program a "random name" generator that conforms to this rule. Note: You may use string functions, but they are not necessary.

Answers

1. Line 20: This may not be illegal, but M$ has previously been defined as a list; it is a good idea to avoid using it as a simple string variable.

   Line 25: Illegal in most systems. A string variable should not be assigned a numeric value.

   Line 40: This is O.K. J is an expression; therefore, it is correct to say STR(J).

   Line 50: This will cause an error. The programmer forgot the quotation mark after the word "DIGITS".

   Line 60: VAL(A$) is equal to 123. So far, so good. But C$ is a string variable and should not be used to hold a number.

Line 62: Nothing wrong here. VAL(A$)/VAL(B$) is an expression and may therefore be used as the argument for the STR function.

Line 65: Perfectly acceptable, but an inefficient way to print A$.

2. Simply use a procedure similar to that we used in Chapter 6 for sorting numbers. If you're having trouble, go back and take another look at it.
3. Here is one method:

```
200   REM -- INDEX SUBROUTINE
201   REM -- A$ IS STRING, B$ MAY BE SUBSTRING
202   REM -- I1 IS INDEX(A$,B$)
205   CHANGE A$ TO A
207   CHANGE B$ TO B
210   FOR I1 = 1 TO (A(0)-B(0)+1)
212     LET J1 = I1
214     FOR J = 1 TO B(0)
215       IF A(J1) <> B(J) THEN 230
216       LET J1 = J1 + 1
218     NEXT J
220   REM -- B$ IS A SUBSTRING
221   RETURN
230   NEXT I1
232   REM -- B$ IS NOT A SUBSTRING
233   LET I1 = 0
235   RETURN
```

```
10    LET C1 = LENGTH(S$)
13    FOR I = 1 TO INT(C1/2)
15      IF SUBSTR(S$,I,1) <> SUBSTR(S$,C1-I+1,1) THEN 30
17    NEXT I
20    PRINT S$; " IS A PALINDROME "
22    GO TO 32
30    PRINT S$; " IS NOT A PALINDROME "
32    REM -- CONTINUE
```

5. The program looks first at the word in the middle of the list. If the word comes later in the alphabet than the searched-for word, the bottom half of the list is removed from consideration. If it comes before, the top half of the list is eliminated. The program then looks at the word in the middle of the remaining half to see if it comes before or after the word it is searching for. And again the list is divided in half. This process is continued until the possible locations have been narrowed down to one.

6. This is one approach:

```
10    REMARK -- RANDOM NAME GENERATOR
12    DIM C$(21), V$(5)
13    REMARK -- READ CONSONANTS
15    FOR I = 1 TO 21
17      READ C$(I)
20    NEXT I
21    REMARK -- READ VOWELS
22    FOR I = 1 TO 5
25      READ V$(I)
27    NEXT I
30    REMARK -- GENERATE 100 NAMES
31    FOR I = 1 TO 100
32      GOSUB 100
33      PRINT C$(R1); V$(R2);
34      GOSUB 100
35      PRINT C$(R1);V$(R2);
37      GOSUB 100
39      PRINT C$(R1)
40    NEXT I
50    STOP
100   REMARK -- GENERATE RANDOM NUMBERS
101   LET R1 = INT(RND(0)*21 + 1)
102   LET R2 = INT(RND(0)*5 + 1)
103   RETURN
```

And here are the data:

```
900   REMARK -- DATA FOR RANDOM NAME GENERATOR
901   DATA "B","C","D","F","G","H","J","K","L"
902   DATA "M","N","P","Q","R","S","T","V","W"
903   DATA "X","Y","Z"
904   DATA "A","E","I","O","U"
```

Chapter 10

String Applications

Many applications require the ability to read strings as data and process them. Programs that enable the computer to understand or execute programs written in new programming languages are classic examples. Some programs of this type are called "interpreters" or "translators" because their functions are quite similar to those of human-language translators.

Actually, the computer can directly understand only its private language, called (not surprisingly) its *machine language*. Humans, however, find it bothersome to cater to the computer by always writing programs in machine language (just as you might find it bothersome to write all your correspondence in Greek). One way to solve the problem is to write programs that function like interpreters. Suppose, for example, you want to teach the computer to accept and execute programs in some other language, like BASIC. Just write a program in machine language that explains to the computer the meaning of each statement in BASIC. This is rather like writing a French textbook in English; the instructions (textbook) indicate the way in which any BASIC (French) statement should be interpreted in terms of equivalent machine language (English) statements. Although you would have to learn machine language, this would be the last time you would ever need to use it! Later, you could add new languages to the computer's repertoire by writing other "interpreters" in BASIC. They could explain the meaning of statements in other languages in terms of equivalent statements in BASIC (which the computer now understands).

Since someone has already written a program to enable the computer to accept BASIC programs, we shall write a BASIC program to teach the computer another language. The program will, of course, use our newly acquired ability to read strings and process them. First, a description of the language.

A New Language: FL-I

The language is one created expressly for businessmen. Its name, FL-I, was chosen because it is a *F*inancial *L*anguage (Version I). A businessman can learn FL-I in a few minutes, then use it to ask the computer questions about some of his prospective investments. A language like this is called a *special purpose language* because the subjects that can be dealt with are limited (in this case, to investments).

FL-I has only six instructions, although others can easily be added. The first one looks like this:

NEW INVESTMENT

When the businessman types this instruction, he wants the computer to ask him for data on the investment he has in mind. The investment might be a share of common stock; if so, the appropriate data would be the length of time the businessman intends to hold it and the dividends he expects it to pay while he holds it. If the investment were a tin mine in Bolivia, the appropriate data would be the length of time the businessman intends to own it and the cash receipts expected during this time. To simplify matters all investments are evaluated at the end of each year.

We will let list Z hold the data the businessman provides for a particular investment. Z(0) will contain the number of years it is to be held. Z(1) through Z(Z(0)) will contain the expected receipts for years 1 through Z(0). For example, if an investment is to be held three years, Z(0) will equal three, and the cash receipts will be in Z(1), Z(2) and Z(3).

The "NEW INVESTMENT" command is equivalent to the following set of statements in BASIC:

```
300    REMARK -- "NEW INVESTMENT" COMMAND
302    PRINT "HOW MANY YEARS OF DATA DO YOU HAVE ";
304    INPUT Z(0)
306    FOR Z9 = 1 TO Z(0)
307      PRINT "WHAT IS THE VALUE FOR YEAR "; Z9;
308      INPUT Z(Z9)
309    NEXT Z9
310    RETURN
```

To state it somewhat differently, when the businessman inputs the string "NEW INVESTMENT", the computer could respond by executing the subroutine above.

A second command in FL-I has the following form:

FIND PRESENT VALUE AT *constant* %

If the businessman wants to know the present value of his investment at a 10 per cent rate of interest, he can say:

FIND PRESENT VALUE AT 10%

The formula used to compute the answer is a modification of the one introduced in Chapter 5. For a three-year investment at 10% it looks like this (where Z1 is the present value):

$$Z1 = \frac{Z(1)}{(1.10)} + \frac{Z(2)}{(1.10)^2} + \frac{Z(3)}{(1.10)^3}$$

In general, for an investment lasting Z(0) years with an interest rate of Z7 per cent per year, the formula can be written as:

$$Z1 = \sum_{Z9=1}^{Z(0)} \frac{Z(Z9)}{(1 + (Z7/100))^{Z9}}$$

As you can see, Z9 is being used as a "year counter"; it starts with a value of 1, is then set to 2, and so on, until it reaches Z(0), with the corresponding terms summed to obtain Z1, as indicated by the sigma (summation) symbol.

When the businessman inputs the string "FIND PRESENT VALUE AT 10%", the computer should first scan it for the interest rate, then find and print the answer. If the string had been stored in S$, the computer could execute the following:

```
400   REMARK -- "FIND PRESENT VALUE AT Z7%" COMMAND
401   REMARK -- PUT ANSWER IN Z1
402   REMARK -- FIRST FIND INTEREST RATE: Z7
405   LET L1 = INDEX(S$, "AT")
406   LET L2 = INDEX(S$,  "%")
407   REMARK -- IF NEITHER IS PRESENT, ERROR
408   IF L1 = 0 THEN 430
409   IF L2 = 0 THEN 430
410   LET Z7 = VAL(SUBSTR(S$, L1+2, L2-L1-2))
411   REMARK -- FIND PRESENT VALUE
412   LET Z1 = 0
414   FOR Z9 = 1 TO Z(0)
415     LET Z1 = Z1 + (Z(Z9)/((1 +(Z7/100))↑Z9))
416   NEXT Z9
418   REMARK -- ROUND OFF AND PRINT RESULT
420   PRINT "PRESENT VALUE IS "; .01*(INT((100*Z1) + .5))
422   RETURN
430   REMARK -- ERROR IN STATEMENT
431   PRINT "YOU DIDNT GIVE ME THE INTEREST RATE. TRY AGAIN."
432   RETURN
```

A third command in FL-I has the form:

FIND AVERAGE RECEIPT

It does just that: it allows the businessman to find the average value of the receipts. Here is an equivalent BASIC routine:

```
500    REMARK -- "FIND AVERAGE RECEIPT" COMMAND
501    REMARK -- PUT ANSWER IN Z2
505    LET Z2 = 0
507    FOR Z9 = 1 TO Z(0)
508      LET Z2 = Z2 + Z(Z9)
509    NEXT Z9
510    LET Z2 = Z2/Z(0)
511    REMARK -- CHECK SWITCH.  IF "ON", DON'T PRINT Z2
512    IF F9 = 1 THEN 520
513    REMARK -- ROUND OFF AND PRINT RESULT
514    PRINT "AVERAGE RECEIPT IS "; .01*(INT((100*Z2) + .5))
520    RETURN
```

The result is stored in Z2. Notice that a special variable (F9) is used as a "switch." When it is "on" (*i.e.,* has a value of 1), the result is not printed. This makes it possible to use the routine to help compute the result for the next command, which is:

FIND VARIABILITY

The businessman might want to know the extent to which his investment receipts vary. So we'll give him the standard deviation of the numbers in list Z. The formula is similar to the one in Chapter 6; only the names of the variables have been changed:

$$Z3 = \left\{ (1/Z(0)) \sum_{Z9=1}^{Z(0)} [(Z(Z9) - Z2)^2] \right\}^{1/2}$$

Since Z2, the average value computed in lines 500 through 520, appears in the formula, we merely call those lines as a subroutine before going to work. But we want only Z3 printed, not Z2. To accomplish this we set the switch (F9) to "on," GOSUB 500, then reset the switch to "off" to avoid trouble later. The routine:

```
600    REMARK -- "FIND VARIABILITY" COMMAND
601    REMARK -- PUT ANSWER IN Z3
605    LET F9 = 1
606    GOSUB 500
607    LET F9 = 0
609    LET Z3 = 0
610    FOR Z9 = 1 TO Z(0)
612      LET Z3 = Z3 + ((Z(Z9) - Z2)↑2)
614    NEXT Z9
616    LET Z3 = SQR(Z3/Z(0))
620    REMARK -- ROUND OFF AND PRINT RESULT
621    PRINT "VARIABILITY IS "; .01*(INT((100*Z3) + .5))
625    RETURN
```

A fifth FL-I command has the form:

FIND GROWTH RATE

A person who wishes to invest in a tin mine, for example, might use this command to find out the average rate at which he could expect its profits to increase over time. One way to estimate the average growth rate is to find the relationship between the logarithm of the yearly receipts and time. An estimate of the relationship can be found by finding a line that "best fits" the yearly data when plotted on "ratio scale" or "semi-log" paper; the slope of the line will be the average growth rate. We use the statistical criterion of "least squares" to find the best fitting line, but since the formula is rather complicated, we shall leave it for the footnote.[1]

The following subroutine might be executed in response to the "FIND GROWTH RATE" command:

```
700    REMARK -- "FIND GROWTH RATE" COMMAND
701    REMARK -- PUT ANSWER IN Z4
702    REMARK -- IF ANY YEARLY RECEIPT IS <=0, ERROR
705    LET  Z5 = 0
706    FOR Z9 = 1 TO Z(0)
707      IF Z(Z9) <= 0 THEN 730
708      LET Z5 = Z5 + (LOG(Z(Z9)))
709    NEXT Z9
710    LET Z5 = (1/Z(0))*Z5
712    LET Z6 = 0
713    LET Z7 = 0
714    FOR Z9 = 1 TO Z(0)
715      LET Z6 = Z6 + (LOG(Z(Z9)) - Z5)*(Z9 - (Z(0)/2))
716      LET Z7 = Z7 + ((Z9 - (Z(0)/2))↑2)
717    NEXT Z9
720    LET Z4 = Z6/Z7
721    REMARK -- ROUND OFF AND PRINT RESULT
722    PRINT "GROWTH RATE IS "; INT((100*Z4) + .5); " PER CENT"
725    RETURN
730    REMARK -- ONE OF YEARLY RECEIPTS IS <= 0.
731    PRINT "I CANT COMPUTE GROWTH RATE. ONE OF YOUR YEARLY"
732    PRINT "RECEIPTS IS LESS THAN OR EQUAL TO ZERO."
733    RETURN
```

1. First, we need to compute the average of the logarithm of yearly receipts, given by Z5:

$$Z5 = (1/Z(0)) \sum_{Z9=1}^{Z(0)} LOG(Z(Z9)) ,$$

where Z9 is again the year counter (running from 1, 2, . . . , etc. up to Z(0)). Then, letting Z4 be our estimate of the average growth rate (*i.e.*, the slope of the line of best fit), we have:

$$Z4 = \frac{\sum_{Z9=1}^{Z(0)} (LOG(Z(Z9)) - Z5)(Z9 - (Z(0)/2))}{\sum_{Z9=1}^{Z(0)} (Z9 - (Z(0)/2))^2}$$

The ratio (Z(0)/2)) is the average "value" of time (Z9). The numerator is the covariance of the logarithm of yearly receipts with time; the denominator is the variance of time.

Since the formula for Z4 requires the logarithm of each item in list Z, the growth rate cannot be computed if any of the values is less than or equal to zero.

The last command is the simplest. It is:

ALL DONE

And here is a routine for it:

```
160   REMARK -- FINISHED
161   PRINT
162   PRINT "BYE NOW."
163   STOP
```

A Note on Investment Data

If you are an investor, you may have realized that not all the commands are appropriate for certain sets of data. For example, if the businessman intends to use the present value command, he may want to include the investment's ending (expected cash) value as part of the last year's data (in Z(Z(0))). Then he can compare the initial outlay with the resulting present value figure. If the former is smaller, the investment should presumably be undertaken.

Obviously, it would make little sense to compute the average value, variability, or growth rate of a set of data that includes both regular receipts and a terminal value. On the other hand, such computations could prove particularly valuable with data indicating the sales of a product over the years, the dividends received from a share of common stock, and the like.

Any investment may be evaluated using all the commands in FL-I. But the businessman might have to input his data twice—once to compute present value and once to compute the other measures.

An Interpreter for FL-I

Among professional programmers, the term *interpreter* has a very specialized meaning. It refers to a program that:

1. Accepts another program written in a language the computer doesn't already understand,
2. Scans each statement to determine which of the set of legal statements it is,
3. Executes each statement directly.

We have already written a set of subroutines to perform the latter function; we can now execute any legal FL-I statement. All we need to complete the interpreter is an "executive routine." It should ask the businessman for an instruction, then scan it to see which routine is appropriate. After that instruction has been executed, the interpreter should ask for another instruction; and so on, until the user types "ALL DONE".

To make things easier, let's add a subroutine to remove all the blanks from the instruction. With it we can allow the user to include as many blanks as he wishes without affecting the interpreter's ability to understand what he has said. This is the needed subroutine: [2]

```
200    REMARK -- REMOVE BLANKS FROM S$
201    REMARK -- X$ IS A TEMPORARY STRING
205    LET X$ = " "
207    FOR Z9 = 1 TO LENGTH(S$)
208      IF SUBSTR(S$, Z9, 1) = " " THEN 210
209      LET X$ = X$ + SUBSTR(S$, Z9, 1)
210    NEXT Z9
215    LET S$ = SUBSTR(X$, 2)
217    RETURN
```

We assumed earlier that the user's instruction was stored in S$, so this routine scans S$. First it initializes a temporary string, X$, to contain one blank. Every nonblank character encountered in S$ is added to X$. After all the characters in S$ have been examined, X$ (minus the initial blank) becomes the new S$.

And now the executive routine:

```
 10    REMARK -- FINANCIAL LANGUAGE (FL-I) INTERPRETER
 11    REMARK
 20    REMARK -- Z IS THE LIST OF DATA ON AN INVESTMENT
 21    DIM Z(100)
 30    REMARK -- F9 IS A SWITCH.  INITIALIZE IT TO "OFF"
 31    LET F9 = 0
 32    REMARK
 40    PRINT "HELLO.  PLEASE GIVE ME SOME FL-I INSTRUCTIONS."
100    REMARK -- ASK FOR A NEW LINE.  STORE IT IN S$
101    PRINT
103    PRINT "WHAT NEXT";
104    INPUT S$
105    REMARK -- REMOVE BLANKS FROM S$
106    GOSUB 200
110    REMARK -- SEE WHAT KIND OF COMMAND IT IS
```

2. The same result could be obtained using the CHANGE statement instead of string addition. Simply CHANGE S$ to a list of code numbers; then set up a temporary list X. Move all nonblank characters from the list containing S$ to X, counting the number moved in X(0). Then CHANGE X to S$.

```
112    IF INDEX(S$,  "NEWINV") <> 1 THEN 115
113    GOSUB 300
114    GO TO 100
115    IF INDEX(S$,  "FINDPR") <> 1 THEN 118
116    GOSUB 400
117    GO TO 100
118    IF INDEX(S$, "FINDAVE") <> 1 THEN 121
119    GOSUB 500
120    GO TO 100
121    IF INDEX(S$, "FINDVAR") <> 1 THEN 124
122    GOSUB 600
123    GO TO 100
124    IF INDEX(S$,  "FINDGR") <> 1 THEN 127
125    GOSUB 700
126    GO TO 100
127    IF INDEX(S$, "ALLDONE") = 1 THEN 160
139    REMARK
140    REMARK -- ILLEGAL COMMAND
141    PRINT "I DONT UNDERSTAND THAT.  TRY AGAIN."
142    GO TO 100
```

The Result

We asked one businessman to try our interpreter. Here's what happened:

```
HELLO.  PLEASE GIVE ME SOME FL-I INSTRUCTIONS.

WHAT NEXT? NEW INVESTMENT
HOW MANY YEARS OF DATA DO YOU HAVE ? 3
WHAT IS THE VALUE FOR YEAR  1? 101.50
WHAT IS THE VALUE FOR YEAR  2? 104.90
WHAT IS THE VALUE FOR YEAR  3? 109.65

WHAT NEXT? FIND GROWTH RATE
GROWTH RATE IS  3 PER CENT

WHAT NEXT? FIND AVERAGE RECEIPT
AVERAGE RECEIPT IS  105.35

WHAT NEXT? FIND WARIABILITY
I DONT UNDERSTAND THAT.  TRY AGAIN.

WHAT NEXT? FIND VARIABILITY
VARIABILITY IS  3.34

WHAT NEXT? NEW INVESTMENT
HOW MANY YEARS OF DATA DO YOU HAVE ? 4
WHAT IS THE VALUE FOR YEAR  1? 2.75
WHAT IS THE VALUE FOR YEAR  2? 3.00
WHAT IS THE VALUE FOR YEAR  3? 3.25
WHAT IS THE VALUE FOR YEAR  4? 105.00

WHAT NEXT? FIND PRESENT VALUE
YOU DIDNT GIVE ME THE INTEREST RATE. TRY AGAIN.

WHAT NEXT? FIND PRESENT VALUE AT 8%
PRESENT VALUE IS  84.88

WHAT NEXT? ALL DONE

BYE NOW.
```

A Translator for FL-I

Now suppose you have your own BASIC program to analyze prospective investments, and you want to include subroutines to find present value, variability, and/or some of the other FL-I features. It would be ideal if you could mix FL-I commands with BASIC commands in your program. In other words we need to add FL-I to BASIC. This can be accomplished by writing a program that translates from FL-I BASIC to ordinary BASIC.

A *translator* is a program that:

1. Accepts another program written in a language the computer doesn't already understand (in this case, FL-I BASIC),
2. Scans each statement to determine which one of the set of legal statements it is,
3. Translates each statement into legal statements in another language (in this case, BASIC).

Here's how our translator will work: It will ask you for a statement in FL-I BASIC. If the statement you give it is a BASIC one, the program will print it as is. If the statement is in FL-I, the program will instead print a GOSUB to a subroutine that contains all the necessary BASIC statements for the desired results. The last statement in your program should be "ALL DONE"; when the translator encounters this, the program will list the BASIC subroutines you need to compute all of FL-I's values. The end result of the translation will be just what you want: a ready-to-run BASIC program complete with FL-I's subroutines for analyzing financial data. On most systems it is a simple matter to direct the output of the translator to the computer's storage; thus you can ask the computer to recall the program and run it later on.

First, since you are planning to mix BASIC statements with FL-I statements, we will require that you put line numbers on the latter. That means we need to write a subroutine (250) to remove the line number from a statement (stored in S$), convert it to a numeric value (for convenience), and store it (in L9) for later use:

```
250    REMARK -- STRIP LINE NUMBER OFF S$
251    REMARK -- STORE IT (AFTER CONVERSION) IN L9
252    LET A$ = "0123456789"
255    LET L$ = " "
257    FOR Z0 = 1 TO LENGTH(S$)
258      FOR Z9 = 1 TO LENGTH(A$)
259        IF SUBSTR(S$,Z0,1) = SUBSTR(A$,Z9,1) THEN 266
260      NEXT Z9
261      REMARK -- NO DIGIT FOUND. MUST BE END OF LINE NUMBER.
262      REMARK -- IF L$ = " ", LET L9 = 0.
263      IF L$ <> " " THEN 270
```

```
264       LET L9 = 0
265       RETURN
266       REMARK -- ADD DIGIT TO STRING
267       LET L$ = L$ + SUBSTR(S$,Z0,1)
268     NEXT Z0
270     REMARK -- REMOVE LINE NUMBER FROM S$
271     LET S$ = SUBSTR(S$, LENGTH(L$))
272     LET L9 = VAL(L$)
273     RETURN
```

Notice how the subroutine works. A string, A$, is initialized to "0123456789". Each character in S$ is compared against every character in A$ until a match is found. This digit is then added to L$, and so on, until the first non-digit is found. Since that must occur at the end of the line number, L$ is then converted to a numeric value that is stored in L9. (We have assumed that the blanks have already been removed from S$ in subroutine 200.) Just for the practice, try playing computer with this routine for S$ = "154FINDPRESENTVALUEAT7%".

Here is our new executive routine:

```
10      REMARK -- FINANCIAL LANGUAGE TRANSLATOR
11      REMARK -- (FL-I-BASIC TO BASIC)
20      REMARK
40      PRINT "HELLO.  PLEASE GIVE ME YOUR FL-I-BASIC PROGRAM."
41      PRINT "ALL STATEMENTS MUST HAVE LINE NUMBERS. ANY"
42      PRINT "STATEMENT FOLLOWING AN FL-I COMMAND SHOULD HAVE"
43      PRINT "A LINE NUMBER AT LEAST 2 NUMBERS LARGER.  IN YOUR"
44      PRINT "BASIC PROGRAM, YOU SHOULD AVOID USING VARIABLE"
45      PRINT "NAMES BEGINNING WITH Z AND LINE NUMBERS BETWEEN"
46      PRINT "9000 AND 9999."
99      REMARK
100     REMARK -- ASK FOR A NEW LINE.  TRANSLATE INTO BASIC.
101     PRINT
102     PRINT "WHAT NEXT";
103     INPUT S$
104     LET T$ = S$
105     REMARK -- REMOVE BLANKS FROM S$
106     GOSUB 200
107     REMARK -- STRIP OFF LINE NUMBER.  IF L9 = 0, ERROR
108     GOSUB 250
109     IF L9 = 0 THEN 150
110     REMARK -- SEE WHAT KIND OF COMMAND IT IS
112     IF INDEX(S$,  "NEWINV") <> 1 THEN 115
113     GOSUB 300
114     GO TO 100
115     IF INDEX(S$,  "FINDPR") <> 1 THEN 118
116     GOSUB 400
117     GO TO 100
118     IF INDEX(S$, "FINDAVE") <> 1 THEN 121
119     GOSUB 500
120     GO TO 100
121     IF INDEX(S$, "FINDVAR") <> 1 THEN 124
122     GOSUB 600
```

```
123    GO TO 100
124    IF INDEX(S$,  "FINDGR") <> 1 THEN 127
125    GOSUB 700
126    GO TO 100
127    IF INDEX(S$, "ALLDONE") = 1 THEN 160
130    REMARK
139    REMARK -- THIS MUST BE A BASIC STATEMENT.  PRINT IT.
140    PRINT T$
141    GO TO 100
150    REMARK -- NO LINE NUMBER. ASK FOR THAT LINE AGAIN.
151    PRINT "YOU FORGOT THE LINE NUMBER.  TRY AGAIN."
152    GO TO 100
```

First, the routine types instructions for entering your program (lines 40 through 46). Then, in line 102, it asks you for a statement, which it stores in S$. After the blanks have been removed (lines 105,106) and the line number stripped off (lines 107 through 109), the executive routine looks to see if the statement is an FL-I command (lines 110 through 127). If so, it goes to one of subroutines 300 through 700, depending on the command. Any statement that does not appear to be an FL-I command is assumed to be a BASIC statement and is printed precisely the way it was input (lines 139 through 141). When the "ALL DONE" command is encountered, the executive routine transfers to line 160, where a STOP command will be printed, followed by all the FL-I subroutines.

The translation of FL-I commands is actually accomplished in subroutines 300 through 700. Here each command is printed as a GOSUB to a subroutine that contains the equivalent BASIC statements. If, for example, one of the commands is:

```
547   FIND PRESENT VALUE AT 8%
```

it would be translated as:

```
547   LET Z7 = .08
548   GOSUB 9100
```

Because the "PRESENT VALUE" command requires two BASIC statements, we have to add one to the line number and use that for the second line. This is the reason for the suggestion that line numbers differ by more than one.

Subroutines 300 through 700 look like this:

```
300    REMARK -- "NEW INVESTMENT" COMMAND
301    PRINT L9;   "    GOSUB 9000"
302    RETURN
399    REMARK
400    REMARK -- "FIND PRESENT VALUE AT Z7%" COMMAND
402    REMARK -- FIRST FIND INTEREST RATE: Z7
405    LET L1 = INDEX(S$, "AT")
406    LET L2 = INDEX(S$,  "%")
407    REMARK -- IF NEITHER IS PRESENT, ERROR
408    IF L1 = 0 THEN 430
409    IF L2 = 0 THEN 430
410    LET Z7 = (VAL(SUBSTR(S$, L1+2, L2-L1-2)))/100
411    PRINT L9;   "   LET Z7 = "; Z7
412    PRINT L9+1; "    GOSUB 9100"
413    RETURN
430    REMARK -- ERROR IN STATEMENT
431    PRINT "YOU DIDNT GIVE ME THE INTEREST RATE. TRY AGAIN."
432    RETURN
499    REMARK
500    REMARK -- "FIND AVERAGE RECEIPT" COMMAND
501    PRINT L9;   "    GOSUB 9200"
502    RETURN
599    REMARK
600    REMARK -- "FIND VARIABILITY" COMMAND
601    PRINT L9;   "    GOSUB 9300"
602    RETURN
699    REMARK
700    REMARK -- "FIND GROWTH RATE" COMMAND
701    PRINT L9;   "    GOSUB 9400"
702    RETURN
799    REMARK
```

The "ALL DONE" command is replaced by a STOP statement:

```
160    REMARK -- "ALL DONE" COMMAND
161    PRINT L9;   "    STOP"
162    REMARK -- NOW LIST ALL SUBROUTINES
163    GOSUB 2000
164    PRINT
165    STOP
```

After the STOP has been printed, your new BASIC program lacks only subroutines 9000 through 9400, which enable you to compute FL-I's results. So subroutine 2000 prints them for you:

```
2000    REMARK -- PRINT SUBROUTINES
2001    REMARK
2005    REMARK -- SUBROUTINE 9000
2007    PRINT
2010    PRINT "9000    REMARK--NEW INVESTMENT"
2011    PRINT "9002    REMARK--Z(0) IS NO. OF YEARS"
2012    PRINT "9004    REMARK--ALL DATA STORED IN LIST Z"
2014    PRINT "9006    INPUT Z(0)"
2016    PRINT "9008    FOR Z9 = 1 TO Z(0)"
```

```
2017   PRINT "9010      INPUT Z(Z9)"
2018   PRINT "9012   NEXT Z9"
2019   PRINT "9014   RETURN"
2039   REMARK
2040   REMARK -- SUBROUTINE 9100
2042   PRINT
2050   PRINT "9100   REMARK--FIND PRESENT VALUE AT Z7%"
2051   PRINT "9102   REMARK--PUT ANSWER IN Z1"
2052   PRINT "9104   LET Z1 = 0"
2053   PRINT "9106   FOR Z9 = 1 TO Z(0)"
2054   PRINT "9108     LET Z1=Z1+(Z(Z9)/((1+Z7)↑Z9))"
2055   PRINT "9110   NEXT Z9"
2056   PRINT "9112   RETURN"
2079   REMARK
2080   REMARK -- SUBROUTINE 9200
2082   PRINT
2090   PRINT "9200   REMARK--FIND AVERAGE VALUE"
2091   PRINT "9202   REMARK--PUT ANSWER IN Z2"
2092   PRINT "9204   LET Z2 = 0"
2093   PRINT "9206   FOR Z9 = 1 TO Z(0)"
2094   PRINT "9208     LET Z2=Z2+Z(Z9)"
2095   PRINT "9210   NEXT Z9"
2096   PRINT "9212   LET Z2 = Z2/Z(0)"
2097   PRINT "9214   RETURN"
2119   REMARK
2120   REMARK -- SUBROUTINE 9300
2122   PRINT
2130   PRINT "9300   REMARK--FIND VARIABILITY"
2131   PRINT "9302   REMARK--PUT ANSWER IN Z3"
2132   PRINT "9304   GOSUB 9200"
2133   PRINT "9306   LET Z3 = 0"
2134   PRINT "9308   FOR Z9 = 1 TO Z(0)"
2135   PRINT "9310     LET Z3=Z3+((Z(Z9)-Z2)↑2)"
2136   PRINT "9312   NEXT Z9"
2137   PRINT "9314   LET Z3 = SQR(Z3/Z(0))"
2138   PRINT "9316   RETURN"
2159   REMARK
2160   REMARK -- SUBROUTINE 9400
2162   PRINT
2170   PRINT "9400   REMARK--FIND GROWTH RATE"
2171   PRINT "9402   REMARK--PUT ANSWER IN Z4"
2172   PRINT "9404   LET Z5 = 0"
2173   PRINT "9406   FOR Z9 = 1 TO Z(0)"
2174   PRINT "9408     IF Z(Z9)<=0 THEN 9440"
2175   PRINT "9410     LET Z5=Z5+(LOG(Z(Z9)))"
2176   PRINT "9412   NEXT Z9"
2177   PRINT "9414   LET Z5 = (1/Z(0))*Z5"
2178   PRINT "9416   LET Z6 = 0"
2179   PRINT "9418   LET Z7 = 0"
2180   PRINT "9420   FOR Z9 = 1 TO Z(0)"
2181   PRINT "9422     LET Z6=Z6+(LOG(Z(Z9))-Z5)*(Z9-(Z(0)/2))"
2182   PRINT "9424     LET Z7=Z7+((Z9-(Z(0)/2))↑2)"
2183   PRINT "9426   NEXT Z9"
2184   PRINT "9428   LET Z4 = Z6/Z7"
2185   PRINT "9430   RETURN"
2186   PRINT "9440   REMARK--CANT COMPUTE GROWTH RATE. LET Z4=0"
2187   PRINT "9442   LET Z4 = 0"
2188   PRINT "9444   RETURN"
2199   RETURN
```

Since these subroutines use only variable names beginning with Z and line numbers above 9000, you can be confident that if you avoid using these variables and line numbers, there will be no conflict.

And that's the translator. The only missing ingredient is subroutine 200, but it can be borrowed from the interpreter. Not only have we added statements to BASIC in an academic sense—we can actually run programs written in this new extended language.

Problems

1. The *internal rate of return* for an investment is simply that interest rate which makes the present value, less the amount invested, equal to zero. One way to find it is as follows: Start with a very low interest rate (say, .1 per cent), and compute the present value less the amount invested. The result should be positive. Then keep increasing the interest rate, recomputing net present value each time. When the latter turns negative, you know that the true internal rate of return is close to the next-to-last interest rate you used. The precision of your result will depend on the rapidity with which you increase the interest rate—the smaller the steps, the more accurate the answer.

   With this knowledge, add a statement to FL-I:

   FIND INTERNAL RATE OF RETURN IF *constant* INVESTED

2. If you are really ambitious, make up a language of your own and write an interpreter (or translator) for it. Or think of some new statements to add to BASIC; then write routines to handle them.

Answers

1. Here is one solution. Add the following routine to the interpreter:

```
800    REMARK -- "FIND INTERNAL RATE OF RETURN IF Z8 INVESTED"
801    REMARK -- PUT ANSWER IN Z5
802    REMARK -- FIRST FIND AMOUNT INVESTED: Z8
805    LET L1 = INDEX(S$, "IF")
806    LET L2 = INDEX(S$, "INVESTED")
807    REMARK -- IF NEITHER IS PRESENT, ERROR
808    IF L1 = 0 THEN 830
809    IF L2 = 0 THEN 830
810    LET Z8 = VAL(SUBSTR(S$, L1+2, L2-L1-2))
811    REMARK -- FIND I. R. R.
812    FOR Z5 = .001 TO .900 STEP .001
813      LET Z6 = 0
814      FOR Z9 = 1 TO Z(0)
815        LET Z6 = Z6 + (Z(Z9)/((1 + Z5)↑Z9))
```

```
816      NEXT Z9
820      IF (Z6 - Z8) < 0 THEN 826
822    NEXT Z5
824    REMARK -- INTEREST RATE IS VERY LARGE
825    GO TO 840
826    REMARK -- FOUND I. R. R.  IT IS CLOSE TO PRIOR RATE
827    LET Z5 = Z5 - .001
828    PRINT "INTERNAL RATE OF RETURN IS CLOSE TO ";100*Z5; "PER CENT"
829    RETURN
830    REMARK -- ERROR IN STATEMENT
831    PRINT "YOU DIDNT GIVE ME THE AMOUNT INVESTED.  TRY AGAIN."
832    RETURN
840    REMARK -- INTERNAL RATE IS NOT WITHIN RANGE
841    PRINT "THE INTERNAL RATE OF RETURN IS VERY LARGE OR VERY SMALL"
842    RETURN
```

Then add these statements to the executive routine:

```
127    IF INDEX(S$, "FINDINT") <> 1 THEN 130
128    GOSUB 800
129    GO TO 100
130    IF INDEX(S$, "ALLDONE")  = 1 THEN 160
```

The necessary alterations to the translator should now be obvious. If not, go back and take another look at it.

One final note for the purist: There may be more than one internal rate of return. This program attempts only to find the smallest one within the range from .1 per cent to 90 per cent.

2. If you get this far, you are doing very well indeed. Even some professional programmers haven't done this.

Chapter 11

Matrix Commands

The commands discussed in this chapter are particularly interesting to mathematicians; in fact, most of these commands were developed especially for them. Don't let this frighten you. Although the terminology may seem strange (mathematicians refer to tables as *matrices* and to lists as *vectors*), the tools of mathematics often have very practical applications. Matrix commands are no exception; you need not be aware of all their mathematical aspects in order to use them. And you will find that they can save you considerable programming effort.

A matrix is simply a table; therefore, all the rules for tables discussed in Chapter 6 apply here. We will only develop some shortcuts for using tables; everything you can do with matrix commands can be done with the tools of Chapter 6.

Initializing Matrices

The MAT (for matrix) READ command provides a shortcut way to read in a matrix. Simply say:

```
MAT READ X
```

This causes matrix X to be filled with data values, row by row. Suppose your DATA statements are:

```
900  DATA 12, 34.5, 27
901  DATA 17, 87.2, 49
902  DATA 91, 45.3, 50
```

Then, if you have said:

DIM X(3,3)

matrix X will be filled as follows:

12	34.5	27
17	87.2	49
91	45.3	50

The computer fills each row, one at a time. If you want X to be filled this way:

12	17	91
34.5	87.2	45.3
27	49	50

write the data:

```
900   DATA 12, 17, 91
901   DATA 34.5, 87.2, 45.3
902   DATA 27, 49, 50
```

You may read more than one matrix at a time; merely separate them by commas:

MAT READ X, Y, Z

Matrix X will be read in its entirety, row by row; then matrix Y, row by row; and finally, matrix Z, row by row.

MAT INPUT works in essentially the same way, except that the numbers are obtained from the program user (and not from data statements):

MAT INPUT A
MAT INPUT A, B, C

The numbers should be input in the order that would be appropriate for DATA statements, had you used a MAT READ instead.

These commands can save you considerable effort. For example, suppose you have dimensioned list X (in a DIM statement) to have ten rows and twenty columns. Then the statement:

10 MAT READ X

is equivalent to:

```
10    FOR I = 1 TO 10
12      FOR J = 1 TO 20
14        READ X(I,J)
16      NEXT J
18    NEXT I
```

And:

```
10 MAT INPUT X
```

is equivalent to the same set of statements with line 14 replaced by:

```
14 INPUT X(I,J)
```

There are other shortcut ways to initialize matrices. If you want matrix R to contain zeroes, simply say:

```
MAT R = ZER
```

If R has five rows and seven columns, it will be initialized to a 5-by-7 matrix containing zeroes in every position. Or you may wish to initialize it to contain all ones. In that case say:

```
MAT R = CON
```

It will now be a 5-by-7 matrix containing ones in every position.

Finally, you may want to create what mathematicians call an *identity matrix.* This is simply a matrix having zeroes everywhere except on the diagonal extending from the upper left corner to the lower right corner, where it has ones. A 3-by-3 identity matrix looks like this:

```
1 0 0
0 1 0
0 0 1
```

A moment's reflection should convince you that only square matrices (those having the same number of rows as columns) can be initialized as identity matrices—merely because only square ones have a diagonal that starts in the upper left and ends in the lower right corner. If you don't believe it, try making an identity matrix out of a 3-row, 5-column matrix:

At any rate, an identity matrix may be created by saying:

```
MAT W = IDN
```

provided W is square.

In many systems MAT READ, MAT INPUT, MAT ZER, and MAT CON may be used to initialize lists (mathematicians call them *column vectors*). If you have a DIM statement that says:

```
DIM X(10), Y(45), Z(7)
```

it is perfectly acceptable to include these statements in your program:

```
10 MAT READ X
20 MAT Z = CON
30 MAT Y = ZER
```

However, a word of caution is in order. Some matrix commands may not work on lists—an error message may be generated. These situations can arise in some systems when you attempt to perform certain arithmetic computations (described in the next two sections). Thus if you plan to use matrix commands on a *list* of items, it is best to define the list as a matrix with one column:

```
DIM X(10, 1)
```

Then if you wish to fill it with data items, write your data statements exactly as you did in Chapter 6. The MAT READ statement will then cause X(1,1) to be filled with the first data item, X(2,1) with the second, . . . , and so on.

On some occasions you may want to create something called a *row vector*—it looks just like a list that has been written across the page instead of down. If you want X to be a row vector with ten items, dimension it as follows:

```
DIM X(1,10)
```

You will see that row vectors differ from column vectors only when it comes to performing arithmetic computations on matrices or printing them. Just be sure to use two subscripts whenever you refer to a list that has been dimensioned as a matrix with one column (or row).

Dimensioning Matrices

The DIM statement tells the computer how much space to reserve for your matrices and vectors. Thus:

```
DIM X(5,3), Y(7,2)
```

specifies that X's maximum dimensions are five rows and three columns, while Y's are seven rows and two columns.[1] So long as you don't exceed these dimensions, you may redefine the size of both X and Y in your program. Suppose you wish to read data into four rows and two columns of X. You may do so by writing the MAT READ command as:

```
MAT READ X(4,2)
```

1. In systems that allow zero subscripts (*i.e.*, row zero and column zero), the maximum dimensions of X would be (5 + 1) rows and (3 + 1) columns, or six rows and four columns. However, in most systems, MAT commands ignore row zero and column zero. If you wish to use them, you should do so explicitly with FOR-NEXT loops.

The computer will then read eight data values and store them in rows 1 through 4 and in columns 1 and 2 of X. The *actual* dimensions of X will then be 4-by-2, although the computer has actually reserved room for five rows and three columns (fifteen items). In fact, in many systems you may also say:

```
MAT READ X(6,2)
```

because only twelve items will be required. In such systems the original row and column dimensions in the DIM statement may be exceeded as long as the *total* number of items is less than the number you have reserved.

You may also specify a matrix's actual dimensions in the MAT INPUT, MAT ZER, and MAT CON statements:

```
MAT Q = ZER(6,3)
MAT P = CON(10,12)
MAT INPUT Z(4,6), A(2,3)
```

In the first case, eighteen items of Q would be initialized to zero; in the second, 120 items of P would be initialized to ones; and in the third, twenty-four values would be read into Z, followed by six values read into B.

The actual dimensions of matrices used in matrix commands must be specified somewhere in your program. If you do not do this with one of the four commands above, the computer will use your DIM statements to determine actual dimensions. And each matrix must be dimensioned explicitly. Of course, if you do not plan to use matrix commands at all, you need dimension a matrix only if its size is greater than 10-by-10 (as indicated in Chapter 6).

Matrix Operations

Arithmetic may be performed on matrices. You can add two matrices by saying:

```
MAT C = A + B
```

In this case, A, B and C must have the the same actual dimensions. If they do, each element in B is added to the corresponding element in A, and the result is stored in the corresponding position in C. If A is a 3-by-3 matrix containing:

```
3   6   2
4   1   5
9   8   7
```

and B is a 3-by-3 matrix containing:

2	4	7
5	3	1
2	5	3

then C will contain:

5	10	9
9	4	6
11	13	10

One matrix may be subtracted from another:

MAT C = A – B

Again, all three must have the same actual dimensions. Each element in B will be subtracted from the corresponding element in A, and the result will be stored in the corresponding position in C.

Matrices may be multiplied:

MAT C = A * B

For this operation to work the number of columns in A must equal the number of rows in B. If earlier you had said:

MAT READ A(4,3), B(3,7)

the multiplication of A times B would be appropriate. The result, C, would be a matrix having four rows (as does A) and seven columns (as does B). In every case where matrix multiplication is possible, the resulting matrix will have the same number of rows as the first matrix multiplied, and the same number of columns as the second. To avoid problems you should make sure that C's actual dimensions have been specified appropriately.

Matrix multiplication has many practical applications. Suppose your company has three salesmen and makes five products. Monthly sales can be recorded in a 3-by-5 matrix (S):

12	17	13	7	2
9	20	15	2	8
4	7	12	14	5

Each row in S represents a salesman; each column a product. Hence, salesman 2 sold nine units of product 1, twenty units of product 2, and so on.

The prices of the products can be recorded in a 5-by-1 matrix P:

$$\begin{matrix} 5 \\ 3 \\ 7 \\ 2 \\ 4 \end{matrix}$$

Do you want to know the total dollar sales for each salesman? Here is a program to do it:

```
10    DIM T(3,1)
20    MAT READ S(3,5), P(5,1)
30    MAT T = S * P
40    FOR I = 1 TO 3
50      PRINT "DOLLAR SALES FOR SALESMAN "; I; "WERE "; T(I,1)
60    NEXT I
70    STOP
```

And the data you'll need:

```
100   DATA 12, 17, 13, 7, 2
101   DATA 9, 20, 15, 2, 8
102   DATA 4, 7, 12, 14, 5
104   DATA 5, 3, 7, 2, 4
```

This is the output:

```
DOLLAR SALES FOR SALESMAN  1    WERE  224
DOLLAR SALES FOR SALESMAN  2    WERE  246
DOLLAR SALES FOR SALESMAN  3    WERE  173
```

The first item (224) in the 3-by-1 matrix T equals the sum:

$$(12 * 5) + (17 * 3) + (13 * 7) + (7 * 2) + (2 * 4)$$

The general rule is this. If T = S * P, the element in the i'th row and k'th column of T is always computed in the following way:

$$T(I,K) = \sum_{J=1}^{M} S(I,J) * P(J,K)$$

where M is the number of columns in S and the number of rows in P. Try this formula to verify that T(2,1) and T(3,1) are 246 and 173, respectively.

It is also possible to multiply a matrix by a single number or by the value of any arithmetic expression. Just enclose the expression in parentheses and place it in front of the matrix:

```
MAT F = (N * (K + 2)) * G
MAT H = (.5) * I
```

The result is the original matrix with each element multiplied by the value of the arithmetic expression. Obviously, both matrices must have the same actual dimensions. If the number by which you are multiplying is 1, you may write:

```
MAT M = N
```

instead of:

```
MAT M = (1) * N
```

Either way, matrix M would end up as a copy of matrix N.

Only one arithmetic operation may be performed in a single MAT command. It is illegal to write:

```
MAT C = A * B - D
```

But you can do the job in stages:

```
MAT E = A * B
MAT C = E - D
```

The same matrix may appear on both sides of the equal sign in statements involving addition, subtraction, or multiplication by a constant, but not in statements involving matrix multiplication. There is a reason for this rule. Think about the following illegal command:

```
MAT C = A * C
```

As each new element is computed and stored in C, one of the original values still needed for subsequent computations is being destroyed! Hardly a satisfactory situation.

Additional Matrix Operations

Two other operations involving matrices can be extremely useful. The first helps solve sets of simultaneous linear equations. Suppose you wish to find values for X and Y that satisfy the following equations:

$$2X + Y = 9$$
$$4X + 3Y = 15$$

Let matrix A contain the coefficients on the left-hand sides of the equations. It will be a 2-by-2 matrix containing:

$$\begin{matrix} 2 & 1 \\ 4 & 3 \end{matrix}$$

Next, let B equal a 2-by-1 matrix containing the constants on the right-hand sides of the equations:

$$\begin{matrix} 9 \\ 15 \end{matrix}$$

Finally, let V be a 2-by-1 matrix containing the unknown values of X and Y. How can we find these values? By using the matrix *inversion* command:

```
MAT C = INV(A)
```

V can be determined directly from C. It is given by:

```
MAT V = C * B
```

After execution of this statement, V(1,1) will contain the value of variable X, and V(2,1) will contain the value of Y.

We shall not go into all the details of matrix inversion. If you wish to know more about it, you should consult any standard college algebra text. However, it should be pointed out that the matrix inverted (in this case, A) must be square. This is equivalent to the familiar requirement that there be as many variables as there are equations. If there are more equations than variables, one equation may be redundant. For example:

$$\begin{aligned} 2X + Y &= 9 \\ 4X + 3Y &= 15 \\ 8X + 6Y &= 30 \end{aligned}$$

(Here the last equation can be derived from the second by multiplying the latter by 2). Alternatively, some of the equations may be inconsistent. For example:

$$\begin{aligned} 2X + Y &= 9 \\ 4X + 3Y &= 15 \\ 4X + 3Y &= 20 \end{aligned}$$

If there are fewer equations than variables, several values of X and Y may satisfy the equations. Here is an example having an infinite number of solutions:

$$2X + Y = 9$$

Even though a matrix is square, it may not have an inverse. This is reasonable enough—some systems of linear equations simply have no solution. It is quite possible, for example, to write a set of N equations having N unknowns and at least one inconsistency. A matrix that has no inverse is termed *singular*; not surprisingly, one that does have an inverse is called *nonsingular*. In most systems the computer will print an error message and quit if you try to invert a singular matrix. In some, however, you can find out whether a matrix is singular after attempting to invert it. If the *determinant* is set to zero after inversion, the matrix was singular.[2] You might thus say:

```
10  MAT C = INV(A)
20  LET D = DET
30  IF D = 0 THEN 100
```

DET is a special function; it assumes the value of the determinant of the last matrix inverted.

The inverse of a matrix is the same size as the matrix itself. In the example above if A is a 4-by-4 matrix, the dimensions of C must also be 4-by-4.

Another matrix operation is *transposition*. Matrix B is said to be the transpose of A if it is a carbon copy of A with the rows and columns of the latter interchanged. Thus:

$$\begin{matrix} 2 & 4 & 7 \\ 3 & 5 & 9 \end{matrix}$$

is the transpose of:

$$\begin{matrix} 2 & 3 \\ 4 & 5 \\ 7 & 9 \end{matrix}$$

If the original matrix has two rows and three columns, the transpose will have three rows and two columns. Since row 1 of the first matrix becomes column 1 of the second, and row 2 of the first becomes column 2 of the second, and so on, you could accomplish a transposition with this program segment:

2. The determinant is a numeric value computed from the elements of the matrix. For present purposes it suffices to know that the determinant of a singular matrix will equal zero. As a practical matter, the inverse is likely to be unreliable if the determinant differs only slightly from zero.

```
60    FOR I = 1 TO 3
65      FOR J = 1 TO 5
70        LET B(J,I) = A(I,J)
75      NEXT J
80    NEXT I
```

But it is much easier simply to say:

MAT B = TRN(A)

Just be sure that the number of rows in B equals the number of columns in A, and the number of columns in B equals the number of rows in A.

Printing Matrices

The command:

MAT PRINT X

will cause the values in matrix X to be printed one per major zone across the output sheet. The items will be printed row by row—first the items in row 1, then row 2, and so on. Should any row have more than five items, additional lines will be required. And when the end of a row is reached, a new line will be started. To illustrate, if X equals:

```
10      47.3      16      7      0.5      32
37      53        98.8    2      0.9      32.15
```

the output would be:

```
10        47.3      16        7         0.5
32
37        53        98.8      2         0.9
32.15
```

If X were a 3-row, 1-column vector containing:

```
10
47.3
16
```

the output would be:

```
10
47.3
16
```

Several matrices may be printed in one command:

MAT PRINT X, Y, Z,

In most systems a comma following a matrix name indicates that each row is to be printed with one item per major zone across the output sheet. Thus the dangling comma in this command is not an ordinary dangling comma. It simply tells the computer to print the items in each row of Z one per major zone. If no comma appears after the last matrix indicated, it will be assumed.

If you want the items more closely spaced on the output sheet, you may write:

MAT PRINT X;

or:

MAT PRINT X;Y;Z;

These statements will cause the items in each row to be printed in minor zones on the page, but each row will begin on a new line.

Semicolons and commas may be mixed:

MAT PRINT X, Y; Z,

In each case the punctuation *after* the matrix name determines its spacing on the page.

Here is a program to solve our set of simultaneous linear equations and MAT PRINT the results:

```
10    DIM A(2,2), B(2,1), C(2,2), X(2,1)
15    REMARK -- READ IN A AND B
20    MAT READ A, B
25    PRINT "HERE ARE MATRICES A AND B:"
28    MAT PRINT A, B,
30    REMARK -- FIND SOLUTION
32    MAT C = INV(A)
34    PRINT
36    PRINT "HERE IS THE INVERSE OF A:"
38    MAT PRINT C
40    MAT X = C * B
42    PRINT
44    PRINT "AND HERE IS THE SOLUTION FOR X AND Y:"
46    MAT PRINT X
50    STOP
```

The output, as you might expect, is:

```
HERE ARE MATRICES A AND B:
 2              1
 4              3

 9
 15


HERE IS THE INVERSE OF A:
 1.5           -.5
-2              1


AND HERE IS THE SOLUTION FOR X AND Y:
 6
-3
```

An Application

To indicate that matrix operations are by no means limited to mathematical applications, we revised the security analysis program of Chapter 6, using some matrix commands. The result was a much simpler program. Here it is:

```
10    REMARK -- SECURITY ANALYSIS PROGRAM
11    REMARK
12    REMARK -- SET UP DIMENSIONS
13    LET N = 10
14    LET M = 6
15    DIM S(10,6),T(10,1),U(1,6)
20    REMARK -- READ IN SECURITY DATA
21    MAT READ S(N,M)
22    PRINT "THIS IS THE SECURITY DATA:"
23    PRINT
24    MAT PRINT S;
26    PRINT
30    REMARK -- PRINT HEADINGS
35    PRINT "SECURITY", "AVERAGE PRICE", "STD DEVIATION"
37    PRINT
40    REMARK -- FIND AVERAGE PRICE, STD DEVIATION
42    MAT C = CON(M,1)
44    MAT T = S * C
45    MAT T = (1/M) * T
47    FOR I = 1 TO N
48      LET T2 = 0
50      FOR J = 1 TO M
52        LET T2 = T2 + ((S(I,J) - T(I,1))↑2)
54      NEXT J
55      LET D = (T2/M)↑.5
56      PRINT I, .01*INT((T(I,1)*100)+.5), .01*INT((D*100)+.5)
58    NEXT I
59    PRINT
60    REMARK -- PRINT HEADINGS
62    PRINT "MONTH", "AVG--ALL STOCKS"
64    PRINT
```

```
70   REMARK -- NOW FIND MONTHLY AVERAGES
72   MAT C = CON(1,N)
74   MAT U = C * S
76   MAT U = (1/N) * U
78   FOR J = 1 TO M
79     PRINT J, .01*INT((U(1,J)*100)+.5)
80   NEXT J
90   STOP
```

This new program produces the same results as the old one and prints the security data as well. We did, however, round the average prices, standard deviations, and monthly averages to make the output easier to read. This is the output for a sample of ten stocks over a six-month period:

```
THIS IS THE SECURITY DATA:

 24.5          30       29.25      27.5          32       31.75
 50      51         52        51         53        52
 37.45         38       39        35.25         34       33.25
 57      56.5           55.75        43.25         40.27         42.8
 42.5          47.5         45         48.75         50.25         49.5
 33.25         33.25         33.25         34.5          35        35
 37.4          38        38.5          39         39        37.25
 25.5          25.75         26         25.5          27        26
 35      36        35.5          36.5          36.77         37.21
 47.8          47.9          47.34         47.25         45.78         43.65

SECURITY          AVERAGE PRICE   STD DEVIATION

 1                  29.17            2.58
 2                  51.5             .96
 3                  36.16            2.12
 4                  49.26            7.22
 5                  47.25            2.71
 6                  34.04            .81
 7                  38.19            .7
 8                  25.96            .51
 9                  36.16            .75
 10                 46.62            1.5

MONTH             AVG--ALL STOCKS

 1                  39.04
 2                  40.39
 3                  40.16
 4                  38.85
 5                  39.31
 6                  38.84
```

Problems

1. What, if anything, is wrong with this program segment?

```
10    DIM X(4,5)
12    MAT READ X(2,3)
13    MAT Y = ZER(3,2)
14    MAT Y = TRN(X)
15    MAT PRINT X;Y;
20    MAT READ X(4,4)
22    MAT Y = IDN(4,4)
23    MAT Z = ZER(4,4)
25    MAT Z = X * Y
26    MAT PRINT X;Y;Z,
30    STOP
```

2. Is this legal?

```
10   MAT READ R(3,4)
20   MAT R = TRN(R)
```

3. Write a program segment that creates a 4-by-4 square matrix having ones everywhere, except on the diagonal extending from the upper-left corner to the lower-right corner. Put zeroes along this diagonal.
4. Write a program segment to solve this set of equations. Include data statements and print results.

$$
\begin{aligned}
4X + Y + Z &= -17 \\
X + 2Y + Z &= -5 \\
2X + 7Y - Z &= 53
\end{aligned}
$$

Answers

1. Nothing. It is legal to redefine the *actual* dimensions of a matrix as often as desired, so long as these new dimensions don't exceed those specified in the DIM statement (or 10 by 10 if no DIM statement is given).
2. No. The transposed matrix will not have the right dimensions to be stored back in R. To avoid the problem, say:

```
DIM S(4,3)
MAT S = TRN(R)
```

3. This is not as difficult as you might think. C is the matrix we want:

```
100  MAT A = CON(4,4)
105  MAT B = IDN(4,4)
110  MAT C = A - B
```

4. Whenever you attempt to solve a set of simultaneous linear equations, make sure the equations are in the proper form. The coefficients for

each variable must represent a single column, and all the constants must be on one side of the equal signs. Since the equations given here are already in the appropriate form, we can set up the data for the coefficient matrix (A) and the constant matrix (B) directly:

```
100    REMARK -- DATA FOR MATRIX A
101    DATA 4, 1, 1
102    DATA 1, 2, 1
103    DATA 2, 7, -1
105    REMARK -- DATA FOR MATRIX B
106    DATA -17, -5, 53
```

The program is virtually the same as before:

```
10    DIM A(3,3), B(3,1), C(3,3), V(3,1)
15    REMARK -- READ A AND B
16    MAT READ A, B
20    MAT C = INV(A)
22    MAT V = C * B
24    PRINT "HERE IS THE SOLUTION FOR X, Y, Z:"
25    MAT PRINT V
30    STOP
```

Only the dimension statement (and data, of course) need be changed to solve any other legal set of equations.

Chapter 12

Programmer-Defined Functions

The most important thing to remember about functions in BASIC is that each represents the value obtained by executing a specific computation. Instead of writing out the computation every time you wish to use it, you simply refer to the appropriate function by name and let BASIC substitute the resulting value for you. For example, recall the arithmetic functions of Chapter 7. LOG(X) represents "the value obtained by computing the natural logarithm of the expression X, whatever the latter might be." As the value of X changes, so does LOG(X). And TAN(X) is the name given to "the value obtained by computing the tangent of expression X." The same relationship holds for the string functions of Chapter 9, although the value obtained may be a string instead of a number. Thus LENGTH (A$) is the name for "the number representing the length of A$," whereas SUBSTR(A$,X,Y) refers to "the substring of A$ starting at the latter's X'th character and having a length of Y characters." And so on—each function names a unique value.

So far, all the functions discussed have had something else in common: They are supplied as part of BASIC. You might call them "canned" functions. Actually there is no reason to limit yourself to canned functions; you can define your own. Such functions are called *programmer-defined functions* (naturally), but in other respects they are like ordinary functions: Each must yield a single value.

The DEF Statement

Suppose you wish to compute the volume of a sphere, given by:

$$V = \frac{4}{3}\pi R^3$$

for various values of R. You could write the formula in a subroutine:

```
100    REMARK -- COMPUTE VOLUME OF A SPHERE
101    LET V = (4/3)*3.1416*(R↑3)
102    RETURN
```

Then if you need the results for two values of R, you could say:

```
50    LET R = 4.5
52    GOSUB 100
54    PRINT "VOLUME OF A SPHERE OF RADIUS "; R; "IS "; V
56    LET R = 27.8
58    GOSUB 100
60    PRINT "VOLUME OF A SPHERE OF RADIUS "; R; "IS "; V
```

But why bother? Since you really want to compute a single value (i.e., volume), why not simply define the formula as a function? You can, by using the DEF statement. First, think of a name for the function. The name must be three letters, the first two of which are "FN". Obviously this restricts you to a choice of one of twenty-six names. Suppose you select "FNV". Then you might define the function like this:

10 DEF FNV = (4/3) * (3.1416) * (R ↑ 3)

Later you can simplify your program:

```
50    LET R = 4.5
52    PRINT "VOLUME OF A SPHERE OF RADIUS "; R; "IS "; FNV
54    LET R = 27.8
56    PRINT "VOLUME OF A SPHERE OF RADIUS "; R; "IS "; FNV
```

Whenever the computer sees the two letters "FN" followed by another letter, it looks for a DEF statement for that function. When it finds the right one, the function is evaluated (like any other expression), and the value is substituted for the function name in the statement in which it was used.

Notice that "FNV" has no arguments. In most systems functions with zero, one, or more arguments may be defined. The computer merely has to look up the current value of R, plug it into the formula, evaluate the latter, and return the value.

You can define other functions, too. Just include a DEF statement for each one. Like canned functions, each may be included wherever an arithmetic expression is legal. Here are some examples:

```
790  LET H2 = LOG(ABS(FNR + FNS)) + (A * B5 * FNN)
792  PRINT FNW ↑ 2; SQR(FNQ)
793  IF FNA < = (47 * FNB) THEN 800
```

Several other points should be made. First, DEF statements may appear anywhere in your program, either before or after you actually refer to a function. Second, the DEF statement is never executed directly; it serves to provide the appropriate formula whenever you refer to the function in *another* statement. Thus it is perfectly acceptable to intermix DEF's with other program statements, as in this program:

```
100   REMARK -- METRIC CONVERSION PROGRAM
101   REMARK -- READ IN CENTIMETERS
104   READ C
105   REMARK -- CONVERSION FUNCTIONS
106   DEF FNI = C * 0.393700
107   DEF FNF = FNI * 0.083333
110   REMARK -- CONVERT CENTIMETERS TO INCHES, FEET, AND YARDS
112   PRINT "CENTIMETERS "; C; "INCHES "; FNI;
113   PRINT "FEET "; FNF; "YARDS "; FNF/3
120   GO TO 101
```

Third, notice another thing about this program—FNF is defined in terms of FNI. No problem. When the computer attempts to compute the value of FNF, it will see that it must compute FNI first and use the resulting value to determine FNF. If you can keep things straight, so can the computer. Just don't let your definitions get circular. Here is an example of what not to do:

```
10  DEF FNZ = (FNY * 100) + X ↑ 2
20  DEF FNY = EXP(W)/LOG(FNZ)
```

Although it is completely legal to use any proper expression in a function definition (including other functions), you should never define any two so that they refer to one another.

Functions with Arguments

DEF statements may also be used to define functions with arguments. For example, the volume function could be defined as follows:

```
10  DEF FNV(X) = (4/3) * 3.1416 * (X ↑ 3)
```

FNV now has a single argument. But why X instead of R? Merely to point out the difference between a *parameter* and any other program variable. Anything appearing as an argument in a function definition is a parameter; usually parameters are restricted to be named by single letters. Hence X is a parameter of FNV. Suppose elsewhere in your program you said:

50 LET V2 = FNV(R)/2

When the computer encounters line 50, it will substitute the current value of R for X wherever X appears in the formula for FNV, compute the function's value, and plug that value into the formula in line 50. A parameter, like X in this case, serves to hold the place of the value you will later specify. You could also say:

73 LET W(I) = FNV(3.5) + (A1 * W7)

or:

159 LET H6 = (FNV(2 * H7)/(2/3)) + EXP(Y)

In the first case, the number 3.5 would be substituted for X; in the second, the value 2 * H7 would be substituted. Whenever you refer to a function in another statement, you may substitute *any* legal expression for the function parameter appearing in the DEF statement.

Parameters have another important characteristic, which is illustrated by this (nonsense) program:

```
  5   REMARK -- FUNCTION DEFINITIONS
 10   DEF FNN(Y) = (1/SQR(P))*EXP((-(.5))*(Y↑2))
 20   DEF FNM(Y) = A*((1 - (Y↑N))/(1 - Y))
100   REMARK -- INITIALIZE VARIABLES
101   LET P = 3.1416
102   READ A, N, X
103   REMARK -- USE FUNCTIONS
104   LET Y = (1/COS(X))*FNM(3.7)
105   LET Z = FNN(0.24) - FNN(0.23)
106   LET W = FNM(Z)
107   PRINT Y; Z; W; FNM(X)
```

Notice that the DEF statements for both FNN(Y) and FNM(Y) specify a single *parameter* (Y). Notice, too, that *variable* Y has been used in lines 104 and 107. Does this mean the computer must use the value of variable Y when evaluating FNN(Y) and FNM(Y)? No. The name given to a function parameter is strictly arbitrary. Since the computer doesn't know in advance what number you will want substituted for the parameter when you refer to a function, you may choose any single-letter name for it. The name you choose has meaning *only* within the function definition (even though it may be the same as the name of a variable used outside the DEF statement).

How does the computer know when you are referring to *variable* Y and not *parameter* Y (or vice-versa)? It's really not so difficult. Look at line 105 of the program. It says: "Compute the value of FNN(Y), replacing parameter Y in the function definition by 0.24. Then compute the value of FNN(Y), replacing parameter Y by 0.23. Subtract the second result from the first, and store the difference in Z." *Only* if line 105 had said something like this:

```
105   LET Z = FNN(Y)
```

would the value of *variable* Y have been used to evaluate the function. Of course, when not evaluating a function with parameter Y, the computer assumes that all references to Y are references to *variable* Y.

Another way to approach the matter is to think of a DEF statement as a tiny program within a larger one. The function may define a special "parameter-mailbox" that only that function can use. Thus, we often call parameters *local variables* because they refer to mailboxes "owned" by DEF statements and not available to the rest of the program. Of course, any variable mentioned in a DEF statement that is not a parameter refers to a mailbox in the larger program. (In line 10, for example, the computer has to go outside the function definition to obtain the value for P.) We often call these variables *global variables*. The distinction is sufficiently important that you should understand it thoroughly.

A function may have more than one parameter; simply separate them by commas:

```
100   DEF FNG(X,Y)       = (X + (2 * Y)) ↑ 3
101   DEF FNH(A,B,C)     = (A * B * C)/SQR((A ↑ 2) + (B ↑ 2)
                           + (C ↑ 2))
102   DEF FNW(L,M,N,P) = (LOG(L + M + N + P)/4) + FNG(3.7,8)
```

Needless to say, you should give the function the right number of arguments when you refer to it elsewhere:

```
500   LET R7 = FNW(R,49,Q(J),A5 * 7)
520   LET T(K,1) = FNG(FNH(2,D,4), 35)
```

The computer will assign each value to its corresponding parameter in the DEF statement. Accordingly, line 520 specifies that the value of FNH(2,D,4) is to be assigned to parameter X of FNG(X,Y), whereas 35 is to be assigned to parameter Y.

Multiple-line Functions

Some systems allow you to define functions whose formulas cannot be written in a single DEF statement. For example, you may want to define the routine that computes the factorial of a number as a function. This is one way:

```
10    DEF FNF(N)
12      LET FNF = N
14      FOR M = N-1 TO 1 STEP -1
16        LET FNF = FNF * M
18      NEXT M
20    FNEND
```

Another example of a multiple-line function is the following, which computes the greatest divisor for any positive or negative integer (whole number):

```
30    DEF FND(M)
32      FOR I9 = ABS(INT(M/2)) TO 1 STEP -1
34        IF M/I9 = INT(M/I9) THEN 38
36      NEXT I9
38      LET FND = I9
40    FNEND
```

When the computer encounters the DEF statements for FNF(N) and FND(M), it assumes they have multiple-line definitions because there is no "=" sign in either DEF statement. Therefore, it looks for "FNEND". Everything between DEF and FNEND is assumed to be part of the definition.

Notice how a value is assigned to this type of function. The function name is used as a kind of "temporary variable" inside the definition. The last value assigned to this temporary variable is used as the value of the function. This is just what you'd want to happen. When you refer to a multiple-line function in your program, the computer will execute the definition (replacing any parameters by the values you specify as arguments), then assign the function whatever value it has when the FNEND statement is reached.

All the other rules for functions apply as before. In addition to parameters, regular variables may be used inside a definition; they are *global* to the program. Thus M in FNF(N) is a global variable, and so is I9 in FND(M). But the function name and any parameters specified are local to the definition. Thus N is local to FNF(N), and M is local to FND(M). In most systems a multiple-line function may have zero, one, or more parameters.

One last point. In some systems you are allowed to define certain variables as local to a function (in addition to the parameters, which are always local). This is sometimes quite useful, especially if you want to avoid altering the values of any global variables inside the function. Thus we might make I9 local to FND(M) by replacing line 30 with:

```
30 DEF FND(M) I9
```

From that point on the I9 used by the function will bear no relationship to the I9 used in the rest of the program.

Several variables may be defined as local with systems that have this feature. Merely place them all at the end of the DEF statement and separate them with commas:

```
100 DEF FNX(S,T) U7, V, R6
```

A Useful Function

Programmer-defined functions can be very handy, particularly if you have a messy formula to evaluate repeatedly. To illustrate, assume you wish to generate random numbers that come from a normally-distributed population having an average value (mean) of zero and a standard deviation of 1. Roughly speaking, this means that if you were to divide the interval between −5 and +5 into many smaller intervals of equal length, generate a great many random numbers, and plot on a graph the number in each interval, you will find that this "frequency diagram" would have a "bell shape." Values close to the mean would occur more frequently than others, with about 68 per cent falling in the interval between −1 and +1.

It is clear that RND can't be used for this purpose because the numbers it generates are *uniformly* distributed and are restricted to values between zero and 1. That means that values around the mean (.5) are no more likely to occur than values very close to zero or 1. But it is possible to transform uniform random numbers into approximately normal ones. Here's a function that does it:

```
DEF FNR(X) = SQR(-LOG(RND(0))) * (COS(6.283185 * X)
+ SIN(6.28315 * X))
```

If you want to know why this function happens to generate random numbers, consult the reference in the footnote.[1]

1. See G. E. P. Box and M. E. Miller, "A Note on the Generation of Normal Deviates," *Ann. Math. Stat.* 29: 610–11.

FNR(X) requires two uniform random numbers; one is obtained within the function, the other must be given when you refer to the function:

LET Z = FNR(RND(0))

To test FNR, 1000 random numbers were generated, and those falling into each of seven intervals (less than or equal to −3, greater than −3 and less than or equal to −2, greater than −2 to less than or equal to −1, and so on, up to greater than +3) counted. The mean and standard deviations were also computed.[2] Here is the program:

```
 10  REMARK -- GENERATE 1000 RANDOM NORMALLY-DISTRIBUTED NUMBERS
 11  REMARK
 20  DEF FNR(X) = SQR(-LOG(RND(0)))*(COS(6.283185*X)+SIN(6.283185*X))
 30  REMARK -- GENERATE NUMBERS AND COUNT FREQUENCIES IN UNIT
 31  REMARK -- INTERVALS FROM -3 TO +3.  COMPUTE MEAN, STD. DEVIATION
 40  REMARK -- INITIALIZE COUNTERS
 41  FOR J = 0 TO 7
 42    LET T(J) = 0
 43  NEXT J
 45  LET T1 = 0
 47  LET T2 = 0
 50  REMARK -- GENERATE EACH NUMBER, ADD TO TOTALS
 51  FOR I = 1 TO 1000
 54    LET Z = FNR(RND(0))
 55    LET T1 = T1 + Z
 56    LET T2 = T2 + (Z↑2)
 57    IF Z > -3 THEN 60
 58    LET T(0) = T(0) + 1
 59    GO TO 70
 60    FOR J = -2 TO 3
 61      IF Z <= J THEN 65
 62    NEXT J
 63    LET T(7) = T(7) + 1
 64    GO TO 70
 65    LET T(J+3) = T(J+3) + 1
 70  NEXT I
 72  REMARK -- COMPUTE STANDARD DEVIATION
 74  LET S = SQR((T2/1000) - ((T1/1000)↑2))
 80  REMARK -- PRINT RESULTS
 81  PRINT "THERE WERE "; T(0); "NUMBERS LESS THAN OR EQUAL TO -3."
 82  PRINT "THERE WERE "; T(1); "NUMBERS IN INTERVAL -3 TO -2."
 83  PRINT "THERE WERE "; T(2); "NUMBERS IN INTERVAL -2 TO -1."
 84  PRINT "THERE WERE "; T(3); "NUMBERS IN INTERVAL -1 TO  0."
 85  PRINT "THERE WERE "; T(4); "NUMBERS IN INTERVAL  0 TO +1."
 86  PRINT "THERE WERE "; T(5); "NUMBERS IN INTERVAL +1 TO +2."
 87  PRINT "THERE WERE "; T(6); "NUMBERS IN INTERVAL +2 TO +3."
 88  PRINT "THERE WERE "; T(7); "NUMBERS GREATER THAN +3."
 90  PRINT
 92  PRINT "THE MEAN WAS APPROXIMATELY "; .01*(INT(100*(T1/1000)+.5))
 93  PRINT
 94  PRINT "THE STANDARD DEVIATION WAS APPROXIMATELY ";
 95  PRINT .01*(INT((100*S)+.5))
100  STOP
```

---

2. The standard deviation was computed with a "shortcut" formula, but the result should be the same as that obtained with the longer formula introduced in Chapter 6. Statistically speaking, a slightly better estimate of the "true" population standard deviation could have been obtained with the following formula:

74 LET S = SQR(((T2) − ((T1 ↑ 2)/1000))/999)

However, because our sample is so large (1000), the difference between the two formulas should be slight.

And here are its results:

```
THERE WERE     1     NUMBERS LESS THAN OR EQUAL TO -3.
THERE WERE     20    NUMBERS IN INTERVAL -3 TO -2.
THERE WERE     125   NUMBERS IN INTERVAL -2 TO -1.
THERE WERE     333   NUMBERS IN INTERVAL -1 TO  0.
THERE WERE     355   NUMBERS IN INTERVAL  0 TO +1.
THERE WERE     141   NUMBERS IN INTERVAL +1 TO +2.
THERE WERE     20    NUMBERS IN INTERVAL +2 TO +3.
THERE WERE     5     NUMBERS GREATER THAN +3.

THE MEAN WAS APPROXIMATELY        .04

THE STANDARD DEVIATION WAS APPROXIMATELY        .99
```

As you can see, 68.8 per cent of the numbers were within one unit of zero —*i.e.*, between -1 and $+1$. Notice, too, that the mean (.04) and standard deviation (.99) are very close to zero and 1, respectively. And the distribution is reasonably symmetric; nearly as many numbers fell below the mean as above it. Of course, this test is not really adequate; a better one would involve generating perhaps 10,000 random numbers, then performing statistical tests on the mean and standard deviation obtained. Other measures could be computed, too. It is often interesting to know if the sequence of numbers generated has a high "serial correlation"; *i.e.*, if the function tends to produce long sequences of numbers that are "bunched" together. The lower the serial correlation, the better. In spite of its limitations, however, the above test does suggest that FNR is quite a good normal-random-number generator.

Problems

1. Write a function that computes the sum of any arithmetic progression having N terms, with the first term F and the last term L. The formula is:

$$S = \frac{N(F + L)}{2}$$

2. Write a function that finds the common logarithm (log to the base 10) of any positive number. The formula is:

$$LOG_{10}(X) = LOG_e(X)\ LOG_{10}(e)$$

   $LOG_{10}(e)$ is a constant; it equals approximately 0.4343.

3. Write a multiple-line function that assumes the value of the smaller of two numbers given to it as arguments.

4. What is wrong with this program segment?

```
20    DEF FNS(A, B)
21    LET FNS = SQR(((B↑2)/4)/(-(A↑3)/27))
22    IF B > 0 THEN 42
30    DEF FNT(C, D)
32    LET FNT = 2*SQR(-(A/3))
34    IF D < 0 THEN 40
36    LET FNT = -FNT
40    FNEND
42    LET FNS = -FNS
44    FNEND
```

5. Suppose that, during the execution of your program, you need to know whether or not the values of two particular variables are both positive. Is it possible to write a function that will determine this for any two arbitrary variables?
6. We now have a function that generates normally-distributed random numbers from a population with mean zero and standard deviation 1. By multiplying any of these numbers by S and adding M, you can create another random number from a normally distributed population with mean M and standard deviation S. Write a function that uses FNR to do this for arbitrary values of M and S. Then show how you might use it to generate and print fifty numbers for M = 100, S = 10.
7. What will the output from this program be?

```
10    DEF FNA(X, Y) = FNB(X) + FNC(X, Y) + Z
20    DEF FNB( W) = FNC( W, 2)
30    DEF FNC(Y, Z) = (Y/Z) - INT(Y/Z)
40    LET Z = FNB( 4)
50    LET Q7 = FNA( 3, 5)
60    LET Q8 = FNC( 3, 2) - FNB( 24)
70    PRINT Q7; Q8; Z
```

Answers

1. Here's one:

DEF FNS(F,L,N) = (N * (F+L))/2

2. This will do it:

DEF FNL(X) = LOG(X) * (0.4343)

3. Very simple. Just write:

```
10    DEF FNM(M, N)
11      LET FNM = N
12      IF M > N THEN 15
13      LET FNM = M
15    FNEND
```

4. It has one function nested inside another. This is not only confusing, it's illegal.
5. Sure. Just let the value of the function equal 1 if both numbers are positive, and zero otherwise:

```
20    DEF FNQ(X, Y)
21      LET FNQ = 0
22      IF X < 0 THEN 25
23      IF Y < 0 THEN 25
24      LET FNQ = 1
25    FNEND
```

6. Define the function:

   DEF FNP(M,S) = M + S * (FNR(RND(0)))

   Then simply say:

```
50    FOR I = 1 TO 50
52      PRINT FNP(100,10);
54    NEXT I
```

7. You really have to work for this one. It's:

   1.1 .5 0.0

Chapter 13

Additional Features

Many systems offer features not described in Chapters 2 through 12. Some of them are not as widely available as those discussed earlier. But many are just as useful; and you might even find some of them indispensable for particular applications.

The ON Statement

The ON statement allows you to test the value of an expression, then branch to any one of several lines, depending on its value. Although you can already do this with several IF statements, the ON statement is often more convenient. It has the following form:

ON *expression* GO TO *line number, line number, . . . line number*

Suppose that the computer encounters this statement in your program:

```
25  ON (X * 3) GO TO 100, 150, 200
```

The expression (X * 3) will be evaluated first. If the value of its integer portion (the whole-number part) equals 1, the computer will transfer to line 100. If the integer portion equals 2, the computer will transfer to line 150; if the value equals 3, the computer will transfer to line 200. Any line numbers may be used; the integer portion of the expression's value will be used to indicate the position in the list where the next line number is located.

You may include as many line numbers (separated by commas) as you wish, as long as they fit on one line. For example, the statement:

```
10  ON VAL(S$) GO TO 37, 39, 68, 802, 21, 705
```

would cause the computer to go to line 37 if INT(VAL(S$)) = 1, line 39 if INT(VAL(S$)) = 2, and so on, up to line 705 if INT(VAL(S$)) = 6.

What happens if the expression is negative or greater than the number of line numbers in the list? In many systems the computer will simply proceed to the statement following the ON statement, but it is a good idea to know enough about the possible values of the expression so that this situation will never occur. Some computers take a dim view of this sort of thing. Unless you know that your computer is tolerant in this regard, avoid saying:

ON X GO TO 10, 20

if you suspect that X might be negative or greater than 2.

Most systems offer the ON statement exactly as we have described it. A few do not offer it in any form. And a few use the form:

GO TO 35, 47, 90 ON (T+J)

This need cause you no problem for GO TO . . . ON works exactly like ON . . . GO TO; only the arrangement differs.

The RESTORE Statement

Have you ever wished you could read the data in your program more than once? You can, with the RESTORE statement.

Consider the following program, which finds the mean and standard deviation of N data values:

```
10    REMARK -- READ THE NUMBER OF ITEMS
12    READ N
13    REMARK -- NOW FIND AVERAGE
15    LET T1 = 0
20    FOR I = 1 TO N
22       READ X
23       LET T1 = T1 + X
25    NEXT I
30    REMARK -- RE-READ DATA TO FIND STANDARD DEVIATION
32    RESTORE
33    READ N
34    LET T2 = 0
35    FOR I = 1 TO N
37       READ X
39       LET T2 = T2 + ((X-T1)↑2)
40    NEXT I
41    LET D = SQR(T2/N)
42    PRINT "AVERAGE IS ";A; "STD DEVIATION IS ";D
50    STOP
```

The first item in the data stack indicates the number of values to follow. The program first reads this item (N), then uses the following N items to compute the average value. The RESTORE command in line 32 tells the computer that the next READ statement encountered should start reading data with the first item in the stack. The first item is, of course, N. After N is read, the rest of the list is read again (in lines 35 through 40) in order to compute the standard deviation.

RESTORE, by itself, always causes the computer to start reading data items from the top of the data stack. Almost all systems allow you to do this. Some even allow statements of the form:

```
40 RESTORE 950
```

This tells the computer to take the next data item from the beginning of DATA statement 950. For example, if your data statements are:

```
900 DATA 4,5,6
910 DATA 7,8,9
950 DATA 10,11,12
```

the first READ statement executed after line 40 will cause the value 10 to be read in, followed by 11, and then by 12.

TAB

TAB looks like a function; but it isn't. It is used in print statements to control the spacing of output in ways the semicolon and comma cannot. It looks like this:

TAB(*expression*)

When it is used in a print statement, such as this:

```
PRINT TAB(17); X
```

the expression inside the parentheses is evaluated. Then the computer will space to the right until it arrives at the corresponding column on the output sheet. In this case the value of X will be printed beginning in column 17.

You can use TAB several times in one statement:

```
PRINT Y; TAB(10); Z, TAB(45); V
```

The expression following each TAB will be printed starting in the column specified. Either a comma or a semicolon may follow TAB. Thus:

```
PRINT TAB(W * 3), X
```

will cause X to be printed in column (W * 3); and so will:

PRINT TAB(W * 3); X

TAB can be used only to space to the right. If you say:

PRINT TAB(5), LOG(Z7)

when the computer is already beyond column 5 on the print line, the TAB will probably be ignored, with LOG(Z7) printed as if you had simply said:

PRINT LOG(Z7)

It is easy to print numbers in columns with TAB. Here is a sample program using only the semicolon to space output:

```
10    FOR I = 1 TO 5
12      PRINT I; I/2; I/3; I/4
14    NEXT I
16    STOP
```

As you can see, the output is not very orderly:

```
1       .5     .33333333    .25
2       1      .66666667    .5
3       1.5    1      .75
4       2      1.3333333    1
5       2.5    1.6666667    1.25
```

But with TAB we can print in columns:

```
10    FOR I = 1 TO 5
12      PRINT I; TAB(10); I/2; TAB(25); I/3; TAB(40); I/4
14    NEXT I
16    STOP
```

providing much neater output:

```
1            .5             .33333333      .25
2            1              .66666667      .5
3            1.5            1              .75
4            2              1.3333333      1
5            2.5            1.6666667      1.25
```

In every system the columns on the output sheet are numbered consecutively from left to right. But some have seventy-five columns, numbered from 0 through 74; others have seventy-two columns, numbered from 0 through 71; others have seventy-two columns numbered from 1 through 72; and so on. Don't let this minor difficulty bother you. It makes little, if any, difference unless you use TAB with a very large number. For example:

```
PRINT TAB(Q7 ↑ 3), Y8
```

where (Q7 ↑ 3) is likely to be larger than, say, 75. In such a case your system's largest column number (*e.g.*, 71, 72, 74) will probably be subtracted from the value of the expression, and the difference used as the column number to which the computer will tab. Needless to say, a little experimentation will enable you to find out what your computer does in such circumstances.

If the value of the expression used with TAB is not an integer, it will be converted to an integer to determine the appropriate column.

Expanded IF Statements

Some systems allow IF statements of the form:

IF *expression comparison expression* THEN *statement*

The statement following "THEN" may usually be any legal statement except DATA, REMARK, FOR, or NEXT. In each case if the condition specified is true, the computer executes the statement following THEN; otherwise, it goes to the statement after the IF command. This allows statements such as:

```
40  IF A = F THEN PRINT "A EQUALS F"
```

Or any one of the following:

```
50  IF Z3 > Z4 THEN GOSUB 400
75  IF (R + W) * 2 < > INT(LOG(Q5)) THEN RETURN
80  IF A > B THEN LET A = B
```

A few systems even allow you to specify the action to be taken if the condition is false, as in:

```
50  IF D = 29 THEN GO TO 1233 ELSE RETURN
```

The statement after "THEN" will be executed if the condition is true; but the statement after "ELSE" will be executed if the condition is false. In this case both statements cause a transfer to some other part of the program, but this is not necessary, as the following program segment illustrates:

```
50  IF X > 0 THEN LET S = 0 ELSE LET S = 1
60 PRINT S
```

Variable S will be set to zero (if X is positive) or one (if X is not positive). Then its value will be printed.

Whenever an IF statement does not cause a transfer to another part of the program, the next statement in line will be executed.

Logical Expressions

Thus far we have encountered two types of expressions. *Arithmetic expressions* are combinations of constants, variables, and arithmetic operators. When such expressions are evaluated, the result is always a number. The other type of expression considered explicitly in earlier chapters can be termed a *string expression.* When it is evaluated, the result is a string of characters.

There is yet another type of expression—the *logical expression.* Its distinguishing characteristic is simple enough: The value of a logical expression is either *true* or *false.*

Previously we described the standard IF statement as follows:

IF *expression comparison expression* THEN *line number*

A more succinct description would be:

IF *logical expression* THEN *line number*

For we have been using logical expressions all along. Consider the statement:

```
IF A > 3 THEN 200
```

This can be interpreted in the following way:

> If the statement "A is greater than 3" is *true,* go to line number 200; if the statement is *false,* continue.

Obviously, $(A > 3)$ is a logical expression. Some other examples are:

```
    B < > 13
(A + B) = (C/D)
    X < 3.5
```

Some systems allow you to write more complex logical expressions. Particularly useful are the relations AND and OR.

For example, assume that you want to go to line 200 if A9 is between 3 and 5. Using simple logical expressions you might have to say something like this:

```
100  IF A9 < = 3 THEN 110
105  IF A9 < 5 THEN 200
110  REM — A9 IS NOT BETWEEN 3 AND 5
```

But the job can be done with one statement, using AND:

```
100  IF (A9 > 3) AND (A9 < 5) THEN 200
```

Note that everything between IF and THEN constitutes the logical expression. It is, in turn, made up from two other logical expressions. The truth or falsity of the overall expression depends, of course, on the truth or falsity of the component expressions. In fact AND is formally defined with a *truth-table* of the following variety:

LE-1	LE-2	(LE-1 AND LE-2)
True	True	True
True	False	False
False	True	False
False	False	False

LE-1 stands for any logical expression; LE-2 stands for any other logical expression. The table simply indicates that the conjunction of two logical expressions is true only if both components are true. This accords with everyday usage of the term AND.

What if you would like to transfer to line 200 if A9 is less than 3 or greater than 5? Nothing to it, if your system allows the OR relation:

```
100  IF (A9 < 3) OR (A9 > 5) THEN 200
```

The meaning of the term OR can also be shown with a truth-table:

LE-1	LE-2	(LE-1 OR LE-2)
True	True	True
True	False	True
False	True	True
False	False	False

In other words, (LE-1 OR LE-2) is true if either one of the two components is true (or if both are true). This accords with most usage of the word OR and with the meaning of the legal term "and/or".

Some systems allow you to get very fancy indeed. But be certain to use parentheses liberally to avoid ambiguity. For example:

```
IF ((A9 > 4) AND (B3 = 5)) OR ((B3 < A9) AND (X = .2))
THEN 200
```

In many cases you may be allowed to do even more than this with logical expressions. But the ability to use AND and OR in an IF statement is likely to prove the most valuable extension to the concept of a logical expression for most applications.

Appended Clauses

Some systems allow you to append one or more clauses to certain statements; the clause or clauses specify the conditions under which the statement is to be executed. A simple (though hardly exciting) illustration is provided by the appended IF clause. For example:

```
100 LET X = 3 IF X < 0
```

The statement "LET X = 3" will be executed if the condition is met (*i.e.*, if X is less than zero). Otherwise the statement will not be executed at all, and the program will pass to the next statement in line.

Obviously, an appended IF clause has the same effect as the IF . . . THEN construction. Thus one might write:

```
100 IF X < 0 THEN LET X = 3
```

Some of the other clauses that may be appended are more novel. For example, consider the following statement:

```
100 LET X = X - 5 WHILE X > = 5
```

This instructs the computer to execute the statement "LET X = X – 5" over and over again as long as X remains above 5. This will eventually set X equal to the remainder that would have been obtained had the original value been divided by 5.

The UNLESS clause indicates that a statement is to be executed unless the specified condition is met. For example:

```
10 PRINT "HI THERE" UNLESS N$ = "MURPHY"
```

Perhaps the most useful type of appended clause is FOR. Let's say that you want to read fifty values into list X. Ordinarily this would require three statements.

```
15  FOR I = 1 TO 50
17    READ X(I)
19  NEXT I
```

But it can all be accomplished with one statement, using an appended FOR clause:

```
15  READ X(I) FOR I = 1 TO 50
```

This is simply a shorthand method for writing FOR-NEXT loops; but it is convenient, nonetheless.

You may be able to save even more effort by using two or more appended clauses. The general rule is this: The right-most clause is considered first, then the next one, and so on. For example, assume that you want to print the entries of table T. The conventional way to do it might look like this:

```
10  FOR I = 1 TO M
12    FOR J = 1 TO N
14      PRINT T(I,J)
16    NEXT J
18  NEXT I
```

But with appended FOR clauses the five lines could be replaced by one:

```
10  PRINT T(I,J)  FOR J = 1 TO N  FOR I = 1 TO M
```

Appended clauses are helpful, though hardly essential. If your system offers them, use them—but with care.

More about LET

The conventional LET statement has the form:

LET *variable* = *expression*

The expression on the right-hand side of the equal sign is evaluated; then the result is assigned to the variable named on the left-hand side.

Thus far we have insisted that every line number be followed by some sort of identification of the type of statement to follow. The computer then knows immediately whether it is to PRINT, GO TO, RETURN, and so on, or if it is about to encounter a REMark, DIMension statement, or the like. The command LET indicates that an *assignment statement* is to follow. And it makes perfectly clear to the computer, the programmer, and to anyone reading the program exactly what is going to happen.

But one can easily tire of writing LET; and assignment statements are used more frequently than any other type. For this reason almost all systems allow you to omit it. Instead of:

```
10  LET X = 3
```

you may, if you wish, write:

```
10  X = 3
```

But be forewarned—this will make your program harder for others to understand. And it may even confuse you.

Sometime you may want to assign the same value to a number of variables. For example:

```
10  LET S1 = 0
12  LET S2 = 0
14  LET S3 = 0
16  LET S4 = 0
```

Most systems provide a shorthand method for accomplishing this. The most common involves repeated use of the equal sign:

```
10  LET S1 = S2 = S3 = S4 = 0
```

The expression on the right-hand side is evaluated; then the result is assigned to the rightmost variable (here, S4); then it is assigned to the next variable (here, S3); and so on.

Some systems use a slightly different construction:

```
10  LET S1, S2, S3, S4 = 0
```

A few systems provide somewhat less help. The best possible solution to the problem may just be:

```
10  LET S1 = 0, S2 = 0, S3 = 0, S4 = 0
```

Whatever the procedure, the goal is the same—to allow you to write your instructions more succinctly.

Files

Most systems provide built-in file storage. The information is usually stored on magnetic disks that rotate constantly at a rather high speed.

But you need not concern yourself with such details. Just think of a *file* as another data stack—a list of numbers and/or strings.

Unfortunately computer filing systems are no more standardized than traditional filing systems. Every one is a little different. Some allow only the simplest kinds of storage and retrieval; others provide all sorts of options.

This is not the place for an extended discussion of various alternatives. Instead we will merely introduce a few fundamental ideas, using constructs from a representative system. Although other systems vary in detail, the general principles are the same.

Because any given user can have many files, each file must be given a unique name. Generally, file names should begin with an alphabetic character and be relatively short (*e.g.*, six characters or less). Before a file can be used with a program, it must be *opened*. The act of opening a file prepares it for use. If the data in the file are to be read, the file should be opened for input. On the other hand, if a file is to be used for output, it should be erased prior to use. Erasure is accomplished by opening the file for output.

To open a file for input requires a statement such as:

```
OPEN "PRICES" INPUT
```

This will prepare the file name "PRICES" for reading.

To open a file for output requires a statement such as:

```
OPEN "VALUES" OUTPUT
```

This cleans out any previous contents of file "VALUES" and prepares the file to receive output. Once a file has been opened for output, it is a simple matter to store information in it. For example:

```
PUT 3.5
```

adds the number 3.5 to the file. And:

```
PUT "BOO", A/C
```

adds the string "BOO" and then the value of the expression (A/C).

When all desired items have been stored in the output file, it should be *closed*. This is simple enough:

```
CLOSE OUTPUT
```

Items may be read from an input file in a manner similar to that used to read items from the regular data stack. For example:

GET A, B9, X(3), A$

This will get the value of A from the input file, then the value of B9, then X(3), and finally, A$. If later the program encounters the statement:

GET X5

the next item in the input file will be assigned to X5.

When all desired items have been read from the input file, simply say:

CLOSE INPUT

To illustrate the usefulness of files, we will construct a small part of an *information retrieval* system. The information in question concerns grades. First, we will prepare a file named "GRADES", containing the following information:

Number of students in the class
Number of examinations given
Name of student
Score on first examination
.
.
Score on last examination
} information for first student

Name of student
Score on first examination
.
.
Score on last examination
} information for second student

.
.
.

Name of student
Score on first examination
.
.
Score on last examination
} information for last student

Here is a program to create the file and obtain the needed information from the terminal:

```
 5  REM -- PROGRAM TO PREPARE A FILE OF GRADES
10  OPEN "GRADES" OUTPUT
20  PRINT "HOW MANY STUDENTS IN THE CLASS";
21  INPUT N
22  PUT N
30  PRINT "HOW MANY EXAMINATIONS HAVE BEEN GIVEN";
31  INPUT M
32  PUT M
40  PRINT "NOW GIVE ME THE STUDENT DATA";
41  PRINT
50  FOR I = 1 TO N
52     PRINT "STUDENT NAME";
54     INPUT N$
56     PUT N$
60     FOR J = 1 TO M
62        PRINT "SCORE ON EXAM";J;
64        INPUT S
66        PUT S
68     NEXT J
70  NEXT I
80  CLOSE OUTPUT
90  STOP
```

After this program has been run, the desired information will be tucked away safely in the file named "GRADES". Barring some sort of catastrophe, it will be there later on, whenever needed, for use with any program.

Knowing this, we can prepare a program to print the grades of any student:

```
  5  REM -- PROGRAM TO FIND A STUDENT'S GRADES
 10  OPEN "GRADES" INPUT
 20  PRINT "WHAT STUDENT ARE YOU INTERESTED IN";
 22  INPUT N$
 30  GET N,M
 40  FOR I = 1 TO N
 42     GET S$
 44     IF S$ = N$ THEN 100
 46     REM -- THIS IS NOT THE STUDENT, READ GRADES AND GO ON
 48     FOR J = 1 TO M
 50        GET S
 52     NEXT J
 60  NEXT I
 70  REM -- STUDENT NOT FOUND AT ALL
 72  PRINT "SORRY -- THIS STUDENT ISN'T IN THE CLASS"
 74  STOP
100  REM -- STUDENT FOUND, GET AND PRINT GRADES
110  PRINT "GRADES FOLLOW --"
120  FOR J = 1 TO M
122     GET S
124     PRINT "SCORE ON EXAM";J;" WAS ";S
126  NEXT J
130  STOP
```

Note that items in the file must be read one by one, even though some of them may be uninteresting (*e.g.*, those read in line numbers 48 through 52).

Once a file of grades is available, all sorts of useful programs can be created to deal with it. For example:

A program to compute average scores for students and/or for the class as a whole.
A program to print the names of students currently failing the course (*i.e.*, with average scores below some predetermined value).
A program to create a new file, using the data from the old file plus any changes entered by the user (*e.g.*, those owing to errors in grading).
A program to create a new file, using the data from the old file plus the scores received on the latest examination given.
A program to determine overall scores at the end of the term, to prepare a list of students ranked from the highest to the lowest score, and (possibly) to assign letter grades.

If each program in the set were truly conversational, the result could (and undoubtedly would) be called a complete grading *system*. And it could be used by virtually anyone.

Clearly, the availability of file storage makes possible a whole range of new applications. Many are tremendously valuable. This is just as well, since file storage is usually scarce and/or expensive. But it is often well worth the cost.

Problems

1. What, if anything, is wrong with each of the following statements?
   (a) ON 3 GO TO 100, 150, 200
   (b) ON X GO TO 100, Y, Z
   (c) ON (−ABS(X)) GO TO 300,400,500
2. Assume that you have 100 numbers in data statements. You want to print them twice—the first time, beginning in columns 1, 10, 20, 30 and 40; the second time, beginning in columns 1, 20, 40 and 60. Moreover, you want to do this without using lists or tables (*i.e.*, subscripted variables) to show your cleverness as a programmer. What would your program look like?

3. Using the IF . . . THEN . . . ELSE statement, write the shortest program segment possible to set variable S to: -1 if X is negative, 0 if X is zero, and $+1$ if X is positive.
4. A well-to-do programmer uses a computer to help him remember important dates. Every morning he types in the month, date, and day of the week. The computer then tells him what, if anything, is expected of him. Here is a partial list of the days that are crucial and the messages to be printed:

day	*message*
any Friday the 13th	BE CAREFUL
July 2	THIS IS YOUR ANNIVERSARY
July 14	IT'S BASTILLE DAY
any Sunday	GO SAILING

(a) Write a program to obtain the month, date, and day of the week from the user, then print any applicable messages. Assume that your system allows logical expressions with AND and OR.

(b) The programmer really has the relevant information stored in a file called "DATES", in the following format:

month
date
day
message

month
date
day
message
•
•
•
month
date
day
message

"NO MORE"

Every entry is stored as a string of characters. If an item is not relevant, an asterisk is used. For example:

```
"*"
"13"
"FRIDAY"
"BE CAREFUL"
"*"
"*"
"SUNDAY"
"GO SAILING"
```

Re-write your program so that it can use this file.

5. Using the file "GRADES" described in this chapter, write a program to add the scores for a new examination to the file. You will first have to create a new file, then copy it back into the old file. Hint: after closing a file used for one purpose (*i.e.*, input or output), you may re-open it again for another purpose.

Answers

1. (a) This is a perfectly legal ON statement, but it is rather silly. The same result could have been obtained by simply writing:

   GO TO 200

   (b) This is thoroughly illegal. You can only GO TO a line number, and Y and Z are variables, not line numbers.

   (c) This may or may not be illegal, but it is dangerous in any event. Because the absolute value of anything is either positive or zero, (−ABS(X)) must be negative or zero. Your system may react to this by simply going on to the next statement. Or it may refuse to go on at all. In the former case, this statement is superfluous; in the latter, it is downright evil.
2. Here's one possibility:

```
10  REM -- READ AND PRINT IN GROUPS OF FIVE
20  FOR I = 1 TO 20
22     READ N1,N2,N3,N4,N5
24     PRINT N1;TAB(10);N2;TAB(20);N3;TAB(30);N4;TAB(40);N5
26  NEXT I
30  REM -- NOW GO BACK TO THE BEGINNING OF THE DATA
32  RESTORE
40  REM -- NOW READ AND PRINT IN GROUPS OF FOUR
50  FOR I = 1 TO 25
52     READ N1,N2,N3,N4
54     PRINT N1;TAB(20);N2;TAB(40);N3;TAB(60);N4
56  NEXT I
60  STOP
```

3. Some systems allow you to use an IF statement after THEN or ELSE. If yours is one of them, you can get the job done in one line:

IF X < 0 THEN S = −1 ELSE IF X = 0 THEN S = 0 ELSE S = 1

A more prosaic approach would use two statements:

IF X < 0 THEN S = −1 ELSE S = 0
IF X > 0 THEN S = 1

4. (a) There is nothing very complicated about this, especially with AND. Here is a program to do the job:

```
10  PRINT "MONTH";
11  INPUT M$
20  PRINT "DATE";
21  INPUT T$
30  PRINT "DAY OF THE WEEK";
31  INPUT D$
40  REM -- CHECK FOR APPLICABLE MESSAGES
41  IF (D$="FRIDAY") AND (T$="13") THEN PRINT "BE CAREFUL"
42  IF (M$="JULY") AND (T$="2") THEN PRINT "THIS IS YOUR ANNIVERSARY"
43  IF (M$="JULY") AND (T$="14") THEN PRINT "IT'S BASTILLE DAY"
44  IF D$="SUNDAY" THEN PRINT "GO SAILING"
50  REM -- THAT'S ALL
60  STOP
```

Note that every possibility must be checked, since more than one message may apply (*e.g.*, if Bastille day falls on a Sunday).

(b) This is almost as straightforward:

```
  5  REM -- GET INFORMATION FROM USER
 10  PRINT "MONTH";
 11  INPUT M$
 20  PRINT "DATE";
 21  INPUT T$
 30  PRINT "DAY OF THE WEEK";
 31  INPUT D$
 40  REM -- OPEN FILE
 41  OPEN "DATES" INPUT
 50  REM -- GET MONTH (OR "NO MORE") FROM FILE
 51  GET W$
 52  IF W$ = "NO MORE" THEN 100
 60  REM -- GET DATE, DAY AND MESSAGE
 61  GET X$,Y$,Z$
 70  REM -CHECK TO SEE IF MESSAGE IS APPLICABLE
 71  REM -- IF IT IS NOT, GO BACK TO READ ANOTHER RECORD
 72  IF (W$<>"*") AND (W$<>M$) THEN 50
 74  IF (X$<>"*") AND (X$<>T$) THEN 50
 76  IF (Y$<>"*") AND (Y$<>D$) THEN 50
 80  REM -- THIS IS AN APPLICABLE MESSAGE, PRINT IT
 81  PRINT Z$
 82  GO TO 50
100  REM -- ALL ENTRIES HAVE BEEN CHECKED
110  PRINT "THAT'S ALL"
115  CLOSE INPUT
120  STOP
```

Lines 50 through 52 read the entry that is normally the month. But at the end of the file, this entry is "NO MORE". When it is reached, the program must be brought to its conclusion; otherwise, the rest of the record is read.

Lines 72 through 76 check to see if the current message applies. It does not apply if any entry from the file that is not an asterisk does not match the corresponding item for the current day. This is not the only way to perform the required tests, but it is a way that does not require a statement exceeding the length of a normal line. Some systems allow statements to continue on a second line (this is usually indicated by altering the normal order in which a new line is begun). If you have such a system, you can write something like this:

```
IF ((W$ = " * ") OR (W$ = M$)) AND ((X$ = " * ") OR
    (X$ = T$)) AND ((Y$ = " * ") OR (Y$ = D$))
                THEN 80 ELSE 50
```

This single (but long) statement can replace the three statements in lines 72,74, and 76.

5. Here's a program that tells the instructor each student's name, then stores away the new grade as soon as the instructor types it. Afterward, the new file is copied back into "GRADES", replacing the previous contents.

```
10  REM -- OPEN CURRENT FILE
11  OPEN "GRADES" INPUT
20  REM -- OPEN A TEMPORARY FILE FOR THE REVISED VERSION
21  OPEN "TEMP" OUTPUT
30  REM -- GET THE NUMBER OF STUDENTS
31  GET N
32  REM -- PUT THE NUMBER OF STUDENTS ON THE NEW FILE
33  PUT N
40  REM -- GET THE CURRENT NUMBER OF EXAMS
41  GET M
42  REM -- PUT THE NEW NUMBER OF EXAMS ON THE NEW FILE
43  PUT M+1
50  REM -- GET THE OLD INFORMATION FOR EACH STUDENT
51  REM -- THEN PUT IT AND THE NEW INFORMATION ON THE NEW FILE
60  FOR I = 1 TO N
62     REM -- GET AND PUT THE STUDENT'S NAME
63     GET N$
64     PUT N$
70     REM -- GET AND PUT HIS OLD GRADES
72     FOR J = 1 TO M
73        GET S
74        PUT S
75     NEXT J
80     REM -- GET AND PUT THE NEW GRADE
81     PRINT "GRADE FOR";N$;
82     INPUT G
83     PUT G
```

```
 84  NEXT I
100  REM -- THE NEW FILE IS ALL SET, CLOSE BOTH FILES
110  CLOSE INPUT
111  CLOSE OUTPUT
200  REM -- NOW OPEN THEM FOR COPYING
210  OPEN "TEMP" INPUT
211  OPEN "GRADES" OUTPUT
220  REM -- COPY INFORMATION FROM "TEMP" INTO "GRADES"
230  GET N,M
231  PUT N,M
240  FOR I = 1 TO N
242     GET N$
243     PUT N$
245     FOR J = 1 TO M
246        GET S
247        PUT S
248     NEXT J
250  NEXT I
300  REM -- ALL SET
310  CLOSE INPUT
311  CLOSE OUTPUT
320  STOP
```

Index